Cambridge Elements

Elements in Forensic Linguistics
edited by
Tim Grant
Aston University
Tammy Gales
Hofstra University

FORENSIC LINGUISTICS IN SOUTHERN AFRICA

Origins, Progress, and Prospects

Russell H. Kaschula
University of the Western Cape

Monwabisi K. Ralarala
University of the Western Cape

Eliseu Mabasso
Eduardo Mondlane University

Zakeera Docrat
University of the Western Cape

Wellman Kondowe
Mzuzu University

Paul Svongoro
University of South Africa

Shaftesbury Road, Cambridge CB2 8EA, United Kingdom

One Liberty Plaza, 20th Floor, New York, NY 10006, USA

477 Williamstown Road, Port Melbourne, VIC 3207, Australia

314–321, 3rd Floor, Plot 3, Splendor Forum, Jasola District Centre, New Delhi – 110025, India

103 Penang Road, #05–06/07, Visioncrest Commercial, Singapore 238467

Cambridge University Press is part of Cambridge University Press & Assessment, a department of the University of Cambridge.

We share the University's mission to contribute to society through the pursuit of education, learning and research at the highest international levels of excellence.

www.cambridge.org
Information on this title: www.cambridge.org/9781009705202

DOI: 10.1017/9781009705172

© Russell H. Kaschula, Monwabisi K. Ralarala, Eliseu Mabasso, Zakeera Docrat, Wellman Kondowe, and Paul Svongoro 2025

This publication is in copyright. Subject to statutory exception and to the provisions of relevant collective licensing agreements, with the exception of the Creative Commons version the link for which is provided below, no reproduction of any part may take place without the written permission of Cambridge University Press & Assessment.

An online version of this work is published at doi.org/10.1017/9781009705172 under a Creative Commons Open Access license CC-BY-NC 4.0 which permits re-use, distribution and reproduction in any medium for non-commercial purposes providing appropriate credit to the original work is given and any changes made are indicated. To view a copy of this license visit https://creativecommons.org/licenses/by-nc/4.0

When citing this work, please include a reference to the DOI 10.1017/9781009705172

First published 2025

A catalogue record for this publication is available from the British Library

ISBN 978-1-009-70520-2 Hardback
ISBN 978-1-009-70516-5 Paperback
ISSN 2634-7334 (online)
ISSN 2634-7326 (print)

Cambridge University Press & Assessment has no responsibility for the persistence or accuracy of URLs for external or third-party internet websites referred to in this publication and does not guarantee that any content on such websites is, or will remain, accurate or appropriate.

For EU product safety concerns, contact us at Calle de José Abascal, 56, 1°, 28003 Madrid, Spain, or email eugpsr@cambridge.org

Series Preface

The Elements in Forensic Linguistics series from Cambridge University Press publishes across four main topic areas: (1) investigative and forensic text analysis; (2) the study of spoken linguistic practices in legal contexts; (3) the linguistic analysis of written legal texts; and (4) explorations of the origins, development, and scope of the field in various countries and regions.

Forensic Linguistics in Southern Africa: Origins, Progress, and Prospects, by Russell Kaschula, Monwabisi Ralarala, Eliseu Mabasso, Zakeera Docrat, Wellman Kondowe, and Paul Svongoro, is the fourth in this last area, the previous three focusing on the development of forensic linguistics in the Philippines, Australia, and China. It is published in 2025 to mark the *International Association of Forensic and Legal Linguistics* biennial conference from 30 June to 4 July, which will be held at the University of the Western Cape, Cape Town, South Africa.

This is the first *Origins* Element to deal with the origins of forensic linguistics in multiple countries from southern Africa, thereby presenting a multinational, regional approach involving inter alia, Lesotho, Botswana, Mozambique, Malawi, Zimbabwe, and South Africa. South Africa alone has many constitutionally protected indigenous languages, including the official languages of Sepedi, Sesotho, Setswana, siSwati, Tshivenda, Xitsonga, Afrikaans, English, isiNdebele, isiXhosa, isiZulu, and sign language. But, as the authors point out, this protection in law does not always play out equitably in the practical use and assertion of the right to use these languages. Interpretation in legal contexts can become challenging in multilignual contexts both per se and in terms of its proper provision in both the courtrooms and the practice of police investigative interviewing. The improvement of police interviewing is also a developing theme of this Element, and in looking towards the future the authors highlight the need for the institutionalisation of the academic discipline, to ensure future work in the area. They point out the different stages of development and sometimes how precarious a foothold forensic linguistics has as a developing discipline, yet how valuable it will continue to be in improving the delivery of justice across the nations of this region.

Overall, this is a valuable contribution to the Elements series, both itself by providing a fascinating insight into Southern African forensic and legal linguistics and in terms of contrasts with other countries and jurisdictions already covered in the growing *Origins* subseries. Forensic linguistics is clearly a new and developing area in this region that has already made valuable contributions to various nations. We look forward to more of the same.

Tim Grant
Series Editor

1 Introduction to African Forensic Linguistics

This Element introduces the study of forensic linguistics, particularly in southern Africa, but also in Africa more generally. Figure 1 depicts the areas that make up the Southern African Development Countries (SADC) region. Africa is one of the most multilingual continents from a sociolinguistic point of view. According to Kaschula and Wolff (2016:2–3),

> [m]ultilingualism (including bi- and polyglossia) is a given fact for most countries on the planet. In Africa alone, more than 2 000 languages are distributed over 54 independent states, ranging between a handful and up to 500 languages within the borders of one national territory. In terms of national language policies, languages, whether indigenous ('endoglossic') or imported ('exoglossic'), are attributed different status, whether *de jure* or *de facto*. On the one hand, there are African countries that live by constitutions that entrench the rights of several 'official' languages for the country, occasionally allowing for regional 'co-official' languages and/or giving so-called 'national' languages special judicial and/or symbolic recognition.

Such aspects of language planning on the continent cannot be ignored when discussing the relationship between language and law or forensic linguistics.

In the past six decades, there has been clear evidence that the discipline of forensic linguistics is, or was, unknown to general linguists, legal linguists, and

Figure 1 Members of the SADC region
Generated by M. M. Kretzer, using 2021 Global Administrative Areas Data.

applied linguists or sociolinguists on the African continent. Now, however, the situation is rapidly changing, with forensic linguistics studies gaining momentum in various parts of Africa. In this Element we will introduce the topic, define the discipline, address the language of record issue in southern Africa, as well as critically debate the state of court interpreting and translation of documentation into African languages, address police interviewing techniques, while also looking at possible future developments in the discipline of forensic linguistics.

One can also begin by way of introduction to look at southern Africa from a sociolinguistic perspective in order to locate the forensic linguistics debate in this Element. Further research has been conducted by Nosilela (2020) where a comparative approach to language planning in relation to Southern African Development Countries (SADC) is undertaken. Nosilela (2020:90), quoting Heugh (2003), notes that 'Language developments in South Africa, have been somehow a little different from the other SADC countries since language policy in this country has been more overt'. According to Heugh (2003:2), 'British efforts to Anglicise South Africa in the early years of the 20th century acted as a catalyst for powerful resistance to colonial policy' unlike other SADC countries that were more welcoming to colonial dominance. The result of the covert post-colonial language policy has been to retain the colonial languages in the interest of national unity 'with the exception of Tanzania and Somalia.'

1.1 Looking Back

The discipline of forensic linguistics is constantly evolving. Although it is not easy to trace its origin, the term 'forensic linguistics' was first used in 1968, gaining traction when a professor of linguistics, Jan Svartvik, mentioned it in an eminent analysis of statements by Timothy John Evans (Umiyati, 2020). The Evans case (1950), reported at Notting Hill police station in the United Kingdom, constituted a serious crime in which Timothy John Evans was convicted of murdering his wife and child. Based on his confession, the court found him guilty and he was executed in 1953. Events associated with the case generated public and media interest, and hence the publication of Evans's confession by the journalist Ludwig Kennedy. It was at this point that Professor Jan Svartvik, a Swedish linguist, took it upon himself to conduct an in-depth analysis of the confession using forensic linguistics techniques. Based on his analysis, Svartvik concluded in 1968 that Evans had not actually made the statement that the police claimed he had made. Evans was later pardoned posthumously, based on Jan Svartvik's findings. (For a detailed account, see Olsson, 2008; Dissake, 2021.) It became apparent that a miscarriage of justice could have been prevented by an application of linguistic evidence, and Jan

Svartvik, made famous through the Evans case (1950), became forever associated with the field of Forensic Linguistics. Since then, forensic linguistics has begun to establish itself as a discipline, with its application proliferating across the globe, particularly in the Global North. The United Kingdom and the United States of America have the highest numbers of forensic linguistics publications to date. (For a detailed account, see Umiyati, 2021.)

1.2 Looking Forward to Africa

In recent years, research in forensic linguistics has grown in the Global South, with Africa among the geographic areas in which research has taken place. In southern Africa, particularly South Africa, the use of stylistic methods for authorship identification is well argued by Hubbard (1994, 1995) in his work on linguistic fingerprinting. In the same vein, Kotzé (2007, 2010) examined authorship identification in defamation cases, discussing opposing perspectives on forensic linguistics. A seminal work by Moeketsi (1999a) on court interpreting explores the complexities of courtroom discourse in multilingual and multicultural settings, and her contribution is well noted in scholarship on legal interpreting. In 'Language Rights, Intercultural Communication, and Law in South Africa', Kaschula and Ralarala (2004) argue that while individual language rights are enshrined in the Constitution, no procedures exist to protect these rights in the public domain. The authors emphasise the absence of intercultural communication in courts, where Afrikaans and the Western cultural paradigm predominate, resulting in linguistic intolerance and communication breakdowns. In South Africa there is now a book series on the topic of forensic linguistics, with Volumes I–IV published from 2019 to 2024, and Volume V, *Documenting Forensic Linguistics in the African Context: Perspectives in Language and Legal Practice* being the current volume which is being finalised and due to be published in 2025. The series name is 'Studies in Forensic and Legal Linguistics in Africa and Beyond' (SF&LLA) (Ralarala, Kaschula, & Heydon, 2019; Docrat, Kachula, & Ralarala, 2021; Ralarala, Kaschula, & Heydon, 2022; Kaschula, Ralarala & Heydon, 2023). These books are published under the auspices of the University of the Western Cape. This university has also approved the setting up of the African Centre for Applied Research in Forensic Linguistics (ACARFiL), which will begin operations in 2025. This builds on the existing institutional Research Chair in Forensic Linguistics and Multilingualism, which was established in 2022, the only one in Africa. During the last decade, we have witnessed an exponential growth in publications in the field, largely from southern Africa. Research has covered a wide range of specialist areas – courtroom discourse, police interviewing and record construction, hate speech, authorship attribution, and legal or court interpreting, as well as language and crime, among others.

In Malawi, studies in forensic linguistics started in 2015 at Mzuzu University, where it was offered as a single module for undergraduate students studying a Bachelor of Education (Language) (Kondowe & Mtanga, 2023). The module was introduced to challenge long-standing traditional approaches to linguistics studies. Later, the University of Malawi started offering some forensic linguistics modules to undergraduate students studying Bachelor of Arts in Law Enforcement and Leadership. A bigger shift was witnessed in 2022, when Mzuzu University introduced a postgraduate programme named Master of Arts in Applied Linguistics (Law Enforcement Discourse) (Kondowe & Mtanga, 2023). The programme has attracted and brought together students from different backgrounds such as linguistics, security studies, law, police, law enforcement, human rights, and communications studies. Wellman Kondowe appears to be one of the leading, if not the leading, scholars in this field in Malawi, having made significant contributions to forensic linguistics research and education in that country (Svongoro & Ralarala, 2024).

In Namibia, forensic linguistics started through the establishment of Forensic Stylistics as part of a Stylistics module in 2017. In that year, the Department of Communication and Languages at the Namibia University of Science and Technology launched a Master of English and Applied Linguistics (MEAL) programme, with Forensic Stylistics forming part of Stylistics under the programme. Forensic Stylistics was concerned with the use of analytical techniques in legal and criminal matters, and involved a forensic stylistic analysis of written and spoken materials to determine and measure content, meaning, speaker identification, or authorship in Namibian legal contexts. Six MEAL candidates (later graduates) and their supervisors ventured to submit Forensic Stylistics research projects for the first time. A study by Ndatyapo (2022) titled 'A Forensic Linguistic Investigation of Witness Statements on Murder Cases at Windhoek Police Station' is an example of developments in the field in Namibia. Ndatyapo, an emerging forensic linguist in Namibia, is now embarking on her doctoral dissertation at the University of the Western Cape. This is a comparative study with the title as follows: 'Researching Defamation of Character: A Forensic Linguistics and Comparative Study of Namibia and South Africa'.

There has been a very slow development of forensic linguistics in Zimbabwe, largely because the discipline has not been established as a field of study in the country. Nonetheless, literature on court interpreting has been prolific. Research on this topic in Zimbabwe has focused on five key themes: the evolution of court interpreting and language rights since Zimbabwe's colonial era; training, employment requirements and the accreditation of court interpreters; the role of court interpreters and their work environment; the language of record and sight translation; and Sign Language interpreting (Svongoro & Kadenge, 2015; Svongoro & Wallmach, 2019; Matende et al., 2022a; Ndlovu, 2023b). Studies in these topics generally concur that the multilingual courtroom in Zimbabwe challenges courtroom communication and potentially affects the administration of justice. The studies further show that Zimbabwe's linguistic context requires that courts provide interpreters for ChiShona, IsiNdebele, and fourteen other officially recognised languages, to ensure that the rights of all persons are protected. In view of the country's multilingualism, courtroom interpreting is a crucial aspect of Zimbabwe's judicial system.

In Mozambique, the notion of access to justice and procedural fairness has been discussed in the forensic linguistics literature, with much of this work focusing on police interviewing as discussed in Section 4 of this Element. Some research concentrates on the narratives of suspects whose Portuguese proficiency is low or non-existent, and the extent to which such people are able to deal with the intricacies of the Mozambican legal system (Mabasso & Heydon, 2022). Other studies have examined the linguistic environment in which police and justice agencies conduct interviews in domestic violence cases in the capital city, Maputo (Heydon & Mabasso, 2018). The findings of this research suggest that there is an urgent need for the development of tools to assist agency staff to explain legal terminology and processes in simple Portuguese or in local languages.

In East Africa, as in many other jurisdictions, most of the work done regarding forensic linguistics is in Kenya. This includes aspects of courtroom discourse, such as the use of performatives (Tyeng'o et al. 2015); speech acts in the courtroom (Mwangi, Kiguru, & Nthiga, 2022); courtroom interpreting (Odhiambo et al., 2013a; Kiguru (2010); and courtroom strategies (Satia, 2013; Kamweru, 2016; Kimani, Satia, & Kembo-Sure, 2022). Work on prison and police discourse remains sparse. On prison discourse, notable work has been done by Satia (2013) in which the author examined the way in which inmates in Kenyan jails use language to construct a positive identity. More recently, this author has examined the ways in which inmates speak about crime (study in press). Although there is no known record of published work on police discourse in Kenya, there is evidence of ongoing research on the subject. Beyond these traditional areas of forensic linguistics, there are works on language as evidence, exemplified by Odhiambo and Orwenjo (2023), who examine the linguistic features of terrorism notes; Kembo and Satia (2017), who explore vocabulary and grammar in hate speech cases in some Kenyan languages, as well as Wambura and Satia (2023), who examine the ways in which language is used to normalise and legitimate violence against women in Kuria as part of female genital mutilation (FGM) songs. Furthermore, new aspects of forensic linguistics, bringing in unique African concepts and perspectives, are being explored. Key among such studies are Satia and Maritim (2022), who examine the ways in which power and meaning are constituted and communicated in traditional African courts among the Arror people of Kenya (Mwangi, Kiguru, & Nthiga, 2022). These authors specifically look at conditions under which provocation may be invoked as a partial legal defence in murder cases involving witch lynching. Ngure and Nganga (2022) examine how male disputants in Agikuyu traditional courts are disadvantaged because of topics referred to by elders in court proceedings, as well as the manner in which the elders preside over matters in the courts.

In North Africa, interest in forensic linguistics in Tunisia continues to grow in different research directions. In fact, Tunisia hosted the first African Regional Conference of the International Association of Forensic Linguists (2014) (12–14 December 2014, Sfax). Triki's (2013) research on narratorial techniques in Tunisian police and court transcripts comes to mind. The study is foregrounded on the techniques of discourse presentation, using Tunisian police and court transcripts as units of analysis, with a particular focus on the extent to which police reports and minutes are faithful to the original. In this study, one of the findings is that errors in transcription potentially have devastating repercussions for the final verdict.

In Algeria, corpus linguistics has received great research interest, particular in the area of forensic linguistics. Research has examined the fact that Algerian Arabic dialects suffer from a lack of relevant speech corpora for speech recognition, and the need for a rich dialect corpus to deal with Algerian accent recognition. According to Zergat et al. (2023), this area is a crucial feature of the field of Forensic Voice Comparison (FVC) systems in Algeria. In their work, 'The voice as a material clue: A new forensic Algeria corpus', Zergat et al. (2023) present a new large-scale forensic Algerian speech corpus called *Sawt El-Djazaïr*. The language of investigation has been studied by Fares (2023), who analyses the linguistic techniques employed by Algerian investigating magistrates during suspect interrogations. In this study, the author concludes that Algerian investigating magistrates make use of conversational management to obtain evidence from criminal suspects. In Egypt, there is also the work of Marwa Mustafa (2020) who analyses terrorist manifestos, particularly those related to the Christchurch massacre in New Zealand.

In West Africa, Ghana, there is research interest in forensic linguistics, evidenced by Ansah and Darko's (2019) work, 'Justice in the mother tongue: The task of court interpreters in Ghanaian law courts.' The findings reveal that court interpreters face linguistic and non-linguistic challenges that result in poor quality interpretation. According to Ansah and Darko (2019), inadequate interpretation is potentially detrimental to the outcomes of trials.

In Nigeria, studies in authorship attribution and identification have gained momentum. Machine learning techniques have improved the accuracy of authorship attribution, with contributions to this field made by Ayogu and Olutayo (2016), Babarinde and Oku (2020), and Modupe et al. (2022). It emerges that machine learning has helped to ensure fair outcomes in intellectual property disputes. The analysis of language variations and stylistics in criminal profiling and authorship attribution is also essential to justice, as shown by Babarinde and Oku (2020). Other studies examine the level of awareness and application of forensic linguistic services in the Nigeria justice system, with specific reference to police stations and courts. The studies reveal a high level of awareness of forensic linguistics in the Nigerian criminal justice system, and confirm that forensic linguistic evidence is admissible in the Nigerian courts (Oguejiofor & Evbuomwan, 2022).

In Central Africa, there is evidence of research in forensic linguistics in Cameroon. Dissake (2021) wrote a seminal text titled *Language and Legal Proceedings: Analysing Courtroom Discourse in Cameroon*, investigating language-related problems that arise in courtroom discourse. In a further study on the topic, Dissake (2022) argues that judicial discourse can potentially grant or deprive liberty to litigants, and that it is essential that the accuracy of courtroom discourse be improved. The findings of the study also reveal that judges' self-assessment methods do not necessarily follow any standard, which can compromise court hearings. Other works in the field advocate for the legal recognition of national languages in all legal settings, with a view to ensuring linguistic accommodation for suspects and convicts with poor language proficiency in both English and French (Atindogbé & Dissake, 2019). In this study on terminology development, the authors dismiss the fallacy that African languages have no capacity to handle legal matters.

1.3 Conclusion

The literature reviewed in this introductory section provides an overview of the progress of forensic linguistics in southern Africa, but also in East, Central, and North Africa, covering a total of ten countries. The review is by no means exhaustive. It is apparent that the development and advancement of scholarship and application in forensic linguistics are gaining momentum and that African scholars are contributing to ongoing research in this field. Some regions are ahead of others, but all regions present interesting, well-documented findings and perspectives, revealing uniquely African insights. With regard to southern Africa, the publication of the series by African Sun Press is an important development. The last book that was published is titled *Language, Crime and*

Courts in Contemporary Africa and Beyond (2023). It contains chapters written by scholars from the following southern African countries: Malawi, Zimbabwe, Kenya, South Africa, Tanzania, and the Democratic Republic of Congo.

The next volume, forming part of the book series 'Studies in Forensic and Legal Linguistics in Africa and Beyond' (SF&LLA), combines the insights of researchers from all over Africa. This volume on language and the law contributes to development in this fascinating field, bringing together four interconnected thematic areas: Forensic linguistic evidence; Forensic linguistics prospects, knowledge and application; Language practice in the legal process and courtroom discourse; and Linguistic justice and pragmatics in Forensic Linguistics. The contributions of many expose the shortcomings in our linguistic legislative framework, with contributors offering practical solutions informed by new approaches and research methodologies to ensure the establishment of a linguistically inclusive legal system.

It is worth noting that regional and continental relationships in the field have shown that higher education institutions across the continent are vigorously tackling language issues in law and the exercise of justice. There is a great deal of interest in African languages and the linguistic and cultural diversity of African work and study environments, which are multilingual. Based on the evidence of so many researchers, it is reasonable to state that Forensic Linguistics education in Africa is essential for enhancing access to justice. This speaks directly to Sustainable Development Goal (SDG 16) which deals with access to justice. Education in this field is key to addressing the many language barriers that currently obstruct access to justice, particularly in post-colonial contexts.

In a nutshell, the field of forensic linguistics in southern Africa is shown, in these pages, to be lively, advancing, and relevant to Africa's needs, while the diversity of excellent research suggests that African scholars are applying the discipline in diverse settings, thus enriching scholarship in the field. The discipline is perhaps better established in southern Africa, with a number of other regions following suit as suggested in this section. In the section that follows the language of record and proceedings in southern African courts will be presented and analysed.

2 Language of Record and Proceedings in Southern Africa

2.1 Historical Development of Language of Record and Proceedings

Although Section 1 addresses the historical development of the discipline of forensic linguistics, it is necessary to outline the historical developments relating specifically to the language of record and proceedings policies of courts. This historical discussion foregrounds the constitutional, legislative, and policy developments.

Southern Africa's history is deeply influenced by colonialism and European domination. This has directly influenced the language of record and proceedings in southern African courts and legal processes. There are seventeen countries in southern Africa with over seventy-two dominant languages as indicated herein. In alphabetical order, these are Angola, Botswana, the Comoros, the Democratic Republic of Congo, Eswatini, the Kingdom of Lesotho, Madagascar, Malawi, Mauritius, Mozambique, Namibia, Seychelles, South Africa, Tanzania, Zambia, and Zimbabwe. In this section we highlight the language of record and proceedings models of the countries we believe are representative of the region, which also have common threads.

Southern African countries were colonised by the English, Dutch, Portuguese, and Germans (in Namibia's case). Countries such as South Africa were colonised by both the Dutch and the English, whereas the rest such as Zimbabwe, Zambia, and Malawi were colonised by the English. There were also the British protectorates such as Botswana, Eswatini (previously Swaziland), and the Kingdom of Lesotho. To some extent they had some autonomous rule, but always under the watchful eye of the British Empire. Angola and Mozambique were in turn colonised by the Portuguese. The result of all of this is that the legal systems in southern Africa are infused with both Roman-Dutch and English law, alongside African customary law. The languages of the colonisers quickly established themselves within these African communities (Kretzer & Kaschula, 2022). The effects of this language planning are still felt in southern Africa today.

One can also look at the historical development of the language of record and proceedings in southern Africa from a sociolinguistic and legal perspective. In summary, the exoglossic colonial languages have been maintained as languages of record and proceedings throughout southern Africa. However, that said, there are some important country-specific and international frameworks that dictate the language of record and proceedings, beginning with the Universal Declaration of Human Rights (1948), which states that in any society there should be no discrimination on the basis of language within legal settings. This is similar to aspirational Constitutions of countries such as Zimbabwe and South Africa. Section 6 of the South African Constitution of 1996 now recognises twelve official languages, including South African Sign Language as of 2023, while the Zimbabwean Constitution recognises sixteen official languages, some of them such as isiXhosa being cross-border languages. There is also the International Covenant on International and Political Rights (1996) where article 14 guarantees the right to interpretation where the accused person is unable to understand the language of proceedings. The Framework Convention for the Protection of Minorities (1995) where it is noted in Article 10, subsection 3 that the rights of minorities are protected in courts of law (Docrat, Kaschula, & Ralarala, 2021).

There are a number of southern African counties such as Kenya and South Africa that are signatories to the above legislative frameworks. However, there is still the dominance of colonial languages as languages of record and proceedings. Malan (2009:41) states that there is an official and unofficial language of record in South African courts. Language used in an official capacity concerns the language of record. The language of record is the language in which the court proceedings are recorded and in which the judgment is written and delivered by presiding officers (Malan, 2009:41). The unofficial use of language refers to the language(s) used by accused persons, litigants, and witnesses (Malan, 2009:41). Official and unofficial usages are related to each other. If there is a monolingual language of record policy in place, an accused person who does not speak or understand the language is then solely reliant on an interpreter. Gibbons (2003:202) states that this can only be disadvantageous to a second language speaker who does not speak the language of the court. According to Cassim (2003:25), it is a fundamental principle that persons not only have access to the courts of law, but they must also be able to understand proceedings.

The South African decision regarding the monolingual language of record also needs to be seen in its historical context where English and Afrikaans were initially the two official languages prior to 1994. In terms of language planning these two languages have been elevated in terms of language status, even after the advent of democracy in 1994 (Kaschula, 2021). In the South African context, even though the Constitution is empowering in terms of multilingualism, in 2017 it was announced that the Heads of Courts had decided to use English as the sole official language of record. Making English the sole official language of record means that the court proceedings are conducted in English, and judgment and sentencing are delivered in English (Docrat, Kaschula, & Ralarala, 2021). Ironically, this decision was taken in the interest of transformation.

2.2 Impact of the Language of Record and Proceedings Policies on Litigants' Language Rights

With the historical development and definitional aspects of the language of record policies advanced above, the focus of this section turns to the practical impact thereof on the constitutional language provisions and resultant language rights of litigants in criminal trials.

2.2.1 Constitutional Language Provisions and Resultant Language Rights in Courtroom Proceedings

The constitutional principles and rights inform legislation, policies, and practices. This is true in most jurisdictions. When languages are conferred with official status in constitutional provisions, it implies that the official languages be used in high-status domains, such as the legal system (Lourens, 2012). A language of record policy for courts is complicated by the fact that the SADC region alone has more than seventy-two dominant spoken languages (Mkhulisi & Du Plessis, 2001:157).

2.2.2 Lesotho

At independence in 1966, Lesotho's new language policy declared Sesotho a national language as well as an official language of the state (Khati, 2001:170). In accordance with Section 3(1) of the Constitution of the Kingdom of Lesotho, the official languages were prescribed in the Laws of Lesotho, declaring a Sesotho and English bilingual state. However, English remains the language used in all high-status domains, including the legal system (Khati, 2001:171).

The language of record in Lesotho courts is both English and Sesotho. Records are primarily kept in English (Khati, 2001:173). The legal system comprises lower courts, Magistrates' Judicial, and High Courts (Khati, 2001:173). Sesotho is used mostly in the lower courts, where African customary law is applied while English is used with the application of the common law system in the Magistrates' Judicial and High Courts (Khati, 2001:173). Sesotho may be used at all courts with the exception of the Court of Appeal, where the language of proceedings and record is English only, to accommodate the all foreign judicial officers (Khati, 2001:173). Interpreting remains available for all witnesses who do not understand English. Professional interpreters do not interpret in Lesotho courts; as a result evidence is often misinterpreted. The non-regulation of court interpreting is evident in many African jurisdictions, which is discussed throughout this Element and in particular in Section 3. Proceedings conducted and judgments written in English advantage the legal professional elite with linguistic competencies in English as opposed to the majority of litigants in Lesotho (Khati, 2001:173). The divide between the constitutional provisions entrenching language equality in Lesotho and the practical application thereof was summarised by Khati (2001:173):

> Although the letter and the spirit of the Constitution provide for the languages to be used on a basis of equality in social services, this is not really the case in practice. Sesotho predominates in aural and oral skills whereas English is

prevalent in reading and writing skills – i.e. in keeping records, which are actually permanent points of reference. In order to change the balance of power more efforts must be made to draft and implement a bilingual policy.

2.2.3 Botswana

The language situation in Botswana is somewhat similar to Lesotho, where English dominates in the legal system. The Constitution of Botswana explicates through Sections 61(d) and 79(c) that English is a prerequisite to being appointed a ' ... member of the House of Chiefs and the National Assembly' (Nyati-Ramahobo, 2001:177). English is subsequently the only language used in Parliament. Setswana was later allowed in parliament with the adoption of a Bill in 1998. Despite the monolingual enforcement of government and the Constitution, Botswana remains a multilingual country with approximately twenty-three spoken languages (Batibo & Smieja, 2000). English remains the language of government, the judiciary, administration, education, and business (Nyati-Ramahobo, 2001:181). Although the Constitution does not declare Setswana a national language, it is considered to be the language of the people, their culture, and pride.

Botswana's legal system is similar to that of Lesotho, with common law courts and traditional courts, with the latter referred to as customary courts (Nyati-Ramahobo, 2001:182). With no clear language policy for the legal system, Section 10(2)(f) of the Botswana Constitution states:

> Every person who is charged with a criminal offence, shall be permitted to have without payment the assistance of an interpreter if he cannot understand the language used at the trial of the charge.

Section 10(2)(f) therefore guarantees the right to interpretation within criminal trials. Witnesses primarily use Setswana within courtroom proceedings; however, all evidence provided is recorded in English (Nyati-Ramahobo, 2001:183). According to Nyati-Ramahobo (2001:184), communication challenges are experienced within courtrooms, not only by witnesses but also by court personnel who are able to communicate more effectively in Setswana rather than English. Both in the Botswana Magistrates' and High Courts, an unofficial monolingual language policy exists with the exclusive use of English as the language of record and proceedings (Nyati-Ramahobo, 2001:184).

Based on the Customary Courts Act (1997), Botswana customary courts do not have a language of record and proceedings policy; however, Setswana is the primary language used during proceedings (Nyati-Ramahobo, 2001:184–185). Customary courts are presided over by village chiefs. It is obligatory for a village chief to be competent in Setswana before being appointed (Nyati-Ramahobo, 2001:184).

2.2.4 Zimbabwe

Zimbabwe has sixteen official languages, conferred through Chapter 1, Section 6 (1) of the Constitution of Zimbabwe Amendment, Act 20 of 2013:

> The following languages, namely Chewa, Chibarwe, English, Kalanga, Koisan, Nambya, Ndau, Ndebele, Shangaan, Shona, sign language, Sotho, Tonga, Venda and Xhosa are the officially recognised languages in Zimbabwe.

Section 70 of the Zimbabwean Constitution states that accused persons should be provided with interpreters, to interpret court proceedings into a language understood by accused persons.

Although Zimbabwe's Constitution recognises and confers official status on sixteen languages, the practical implementation and application of the provisions remain lacking. According to Svongoro and Wallmach (2022:145), criminal trials in Zimbabwe are conducted in English, the language of the court. All documents and exhibits are presented to the court in English. Witnesses in criminal trials are not proficient in English, nor are they comfortable communicating in English within courtrooms (Svongoro & Wallmach, 2022:145). With interpretation a guaranteed constitutional right, interpreters are also required to interpret exhibits and other court documents into the languages of all parties to court (Svongoro & Wallmach, 2022:145). Interpreters are therefore required to ' ... shift from short, consecutive oral interpretation to a hybrid, interlingual operation called sight translation' (Svongoro & Wallmach, 2022:145). Sight translation, also known as sight interpreting, is the ' ... oral translation of a written document and is combination of translation and interpretation' (Svongoro & Wallmach, 2022:145).

2.2.5 South Africa

South Africa is no different from Lesotho, Botswana, and Zimbabwe, when it comes to language usage in courtrooms within multilingual societies. The South African Constitution (1996) provides a linguistic blueprint under Section 6 that informs the language rights. Section 6 confers official status on the previously marginalised indigenous languages and obligates government to use the official languages on an equitable basis.

(1) The official languages of the Republic are Sepedi, Sesotho, Setswana, siSwati, Tshivenda, Xitsonga, Afrikaans, English, isiNdebele, isiXhosa, isiZulu, and sign language.

(2) Recognising the historically diminished use and status of the indigenous languages of our people, the state must take practical and positive measures to elevate the status and advance the use of these languages.

(3) (a) The national government and provincial governments may use any particular official languages for the purposes of government, taking into account usage, practicality, expense, regional circumstances and the balance of the needs of the and preferences of the population as a whole or in the province concerned; but the national government must use at least two official languages.

(4) The national government and provincial governments, by legislative and other measures, must regulate and monitor their use of official languages. Without detracting from the provisions of subsection (2), all languages must enjoy parity of esteem and must be treated equitably.

Against this linguistic blueprint, the Bill of Rights, houses the specific individual and community rights. Section 35 of the Constitution (1996) is relevant to this Element, concerning the rights of accused, arrested, and detained persons. Section 35 states the following with regard to language rights:

(1) Every accused person has a right to a fair trial, which includes the right-
  (f) to choose, and be represented by, a legal practitioner, and to be informed of this right promptly;
  (g) to have a legal practitioner assigned to the accused person by the state and at state expense, if substantial injustice would otherwise result, and to be informed of this right promptly;
  (k) to be tried in a language that the accused person understands or, if that is not practicable, to have the proceedings interpreted in that language;

(2) Whenever this section requires information to be given to a person, that information must be given in a language that the person understands.

Section 6 does not confer language rights but informs the provisions of the Bill of Rights. Thus, the two sections must be read together, creating a clear obligation that the nine indigenous languages be elevated in status to ensure equitability alongside English and Afrikaans in practice. Arguments have been advanced where the constitutional language provisions have been said to be theoretical in nature, lacking practicality, discretionary, and vague while allowing for the default position of English and Afrikaans to be selected on the basis of budgetary constraints (Perry, 2004:131; Docrat, 2019).

The majority of case law in South Africa concerning litigant's language rights have centred around the scope of Section 35(3)(k) of the Constitution. While the right does not entrench a language of choice, it does provide for proceedings to be conducted in a language the accused person fully understands (Cassim, 2003:25).

Where that is not practicable, interpretation must be provided. In the case of *State v. Ngubane* (1995) and reaffirmed in the case of *State v. Siyotula* (2003), the court confirmed that the term 'understand' in Section 35(3)(k) meant full comprehension and not partial understanding. Docrat, Kaschula, and Ralarala (2021) have argued that Section 35(3)(k) provides an interpretational right for speakers of the twelve official languages, but a language right for English-speaking accused persons. This is a result of the English monolingual language of record policy that has been in place since 2017.

The monolingual language of record policy dictates that English be the language of record in all High Courts (civil and criminal trials) and that all documents be submitted to the court in English. By implication the language of record policy also affects the lower court proceedings where English is also the sole official language of record. Interpretation is provided for witnesses to impart evidence in a language they understand. The interpreted English version of witnesses' testimony is recorded and appears in the record for appeal and review processes. The policy has several implications on the language rights of litigants.

There have been varying decisions on the scope and application of the constitutional language provisions and rights in courts. In the case of *State v. Lesaena* (1993), the centrality of language was reaffirmed by the court as part of the right to a fair trial, where Mohammed J (1993:265) stated the following:

> ... accorded the fairest and fullest opportunity to articulate his defence, to marshal his submissions and to present his evidence to the court with the most effective linguistic and intellectual resources at his command.

The court stated further that interference with the right would result in a subversion of the right to a fair trial and that procedural irregularity would result in a fundamental injustice.

As with other jurisdictions, interpretation is unregulated. Court interpreters are not required to have any formal qualifications before being appointed (De Vries & Docrat, 2022). There are varying levels of interpreters, and their skill, competency, and proficiency directly affect the quality and accuracy of interpretation in courts (Namakula, 2019). In the case of *State v. Ndala* (1996), the court held that 'competent interpreters are those who are able to give a true and correct interpretation of the evidence'. The high-profile cases of *State v. Pistorius* (2014) and *State v. Van Breda* (2019) shone the spotlight on poor quality interpretation.

The right to interpretation is fundamental in a multilingual society, where the legal system has a monolingual language policy that excludes the majority of litigants from being heard directly in their mother tongue. The right to interpretation was not safeguarded in the case of *State* v. *Manzini* (2007), where an isiZulu-speaking accused person was solely reliant on inaccurate interpretation. A chief interpreter within the court agreed that the quality of interpretation was 'alarmingly poor' with 'numerous errors'. The magistrate incorrectly held that this did not affect the outcome of the case, nor his reasoning and guilty verdict. On appeal, the court held that the accused's credibility could not be assessed where the interpretation was inaccurate. The magistrate therefore failed to recognise the important role of language as part of the right to a fair trial.

The indigenous languages have been used successfully as languages of record and proceedings where it was practical do so and subvert postponements due to the unavailability and shortage of court interpreters as evidenced in the case of *State* v. *Matomela* (1998). The entire trial was conducted in isiXhosa, where the parties before court, legal representatives, and judicial officer were all competent in isiXhosa. Following several postponements due to the unavailability of an interpreter, the case of *State* v. *Damoyi* (2004) also proceeded in isiXhosa, given that it was practical do so. Yekiso J stated that for appeal and review processes it would be easier to proceed with one language, namely English, as interpretation was permitted for accused persons.

In the case of *State* v. *Manzini* (2007) the trial proceeded in isiZulu; upon review, the Judge questioned why an interpreter was not used. The magistrate explained that all parties before court spoke isiZulu; isiZulu was one of the official languages, and the Constitution prescribed that the languages be used equally; isiZulu was the majority spoken language in the area in which the court was seated.

The cases of *State* v. *Gordon* (2018) and M Oosthuizen, *and A Van Straten* v. *The State* (2024) followed the 2017 monolingual language of record policy. The case of *Gordon* was heard in an area with the majority of persons speaking Afrikaans as their mother tongue. The case commenced before the 2017 language of record policy came into effect; however, it concluded afterwards. On review Thulare AJ (as he was then) insisted that the magistrate should have conducted the trial in English and ensure an interpreter was provided. Thulare AJ stated that the monolingual language of record policy had to be applied as it was practical given the current linguistic composition of South Africa, specifically the judiciary. He stated that the appointment of judges to cases on the basis of linguistic competency would result in 'judges being shopped for on the basis of race'. He stated that it was costly to translate judgments into English for review and appeal processes. He said that previous research conducted by Docrat (2017) on the language of record policy was from an academic perspective, where judges did not have this luxury but rather to apply the constitutional provisions.

Similarly, in the cases of M Oosthuizen *and A Van Straten* v. *The State* (2024), grouped together under one application, Tokoto J argued that the language of record policy had to be enforced at all costs and that it was impractical to proceed in any language other than English. He stated that the indigenous languages were not intellectualised at any level for use in high-status domains and that they were particularly difficult to acquire as opposed to English.

Magistrates in the aforementioned cases have proceeded practically and enforced the language provisions and language rights within courtroom discourse. The indigenous languages and Afrikaans have been used equally alongside English, proof that the languages are in fact intellectualised and can be used in high-status domains such as the legal system. Further consolidation of using the languages equally alongside English was evidenced in the bilingual judgment of Maya JP (as she was then), in the case of *Afriforum NPC* v. *Chairperson of the Council of the University of South Africa & Others* (2020). English and isiXhosa were used alongside each, adopting the Canadian bilingual model in the province of New Brunswick. This speaks not only to the intellectualisation of the African languages, but also complying with the constitutional mandate of developing, promoting and using the indigenous languages to reverse the past historical discrimination.

2.3 Futuristic Language of Record Policies for Southern Africa

There is a need to develop regional language policies for courts, to accommodate the official languages and the speakers of those languages (Docrat, Kaschula, & Ralarala, 2021). This balancing act would give effective meaning to the Constitutional language rights provisions and the practicalities of using multiple languages within various courts in a single country. This will require a number of actions to be taken through a consultative process between all stakeholders; this would avoid the current monolingual language of record top-down policy. The new language of proceedings and record policies would need to be informed by statistics emanating from various language audits of the judiciary, National Prosecuting Authority, Law Societies, and the annual general census language demographics. This would need to be revised on a five-yearly basis to accommodate language demographic changes.

It is short-sighted to associate language with race by assuming that the indigenous languages can only be spoken by Black people; that itself is a racial policy that needs to be circumvented. Through the discussions earlier, it is clear that current and prospective judges need to undergo language sensitivity and awareness courses as part of judicial training. This should happen on a continuous basis regardless of linguistic competencies.

2.4 Conclusion

The indigenous languages must continuously be used for bilingual judgment writing purposes to ensure the development of the languages, while also promoting and developing the languages in accordance with the constitutional provisions as well as for the purpose of fostering language equality and inclusivity of all official language speakers accessing the legal system. It may be that in time the pendulum in southern African courts may swing back to a more multilingual and inclusive language of record and proceedings. There are many similarities in existence across jurisdictions. Some country's legal systems could benefit by looking at successful models that could be emulated and adapted. There may also be a need for heads of judiciaries to discuss similarities and differences in order to assess the best way forward in formulating a language policy and language practices that positively affect the rights of the majority. In the section that follows, issues pertaining to legal interpreting in southern Africa will be discussed.

3 Legal Interpreting in Southern Africa

3.1 Introduction

This systematic literature review-based section analyses and evaluates the literature available on legal interpreting in four southern African countries. By so doing, the direction provides a firm foundation for advancing knowledge and suggesting policy changes to improve the profession and practice of legal interpreting and, hence, access to justice for citizens in the selected countries. Broadly, legal interpreting is a branch of interpreting conducted when speakers of different languages have to communicate in legal or paralegal settings (Stern, 2011). Although legal interpreting takes place in different contexts, this section focuses on a specific type of legal interpreting that is court interpreting. This section concentrates on court interpreting situations in four countries from southern Africa, namely Zimbabwe, South Africa, Malawi, and Mozambique. As observed from the literature searched, although similarities exist in the legal systems of the selected countries, it is important to note that each legal system has its own unique court procedures, requirements for court interpreters, and legal concepts and terms that sometimes have no equivalent in other languages (Moeketsi, 1999a, 1999b; Moeketsi & Wallmach, 2005). Southern Africa's linguistic situation, where colonial languages are used as court languages, leads to a high demand for court interpreting. Most cases require language mediation, as suspects are often not competent speakers of the court's languages. Magistrates' Courts, where most criminal cases occur, primarily require interpreting in minority languages like English, Afrikaans, and Portuguese. This linguistic chaos poses challenges for interpreters, witnesses, and suspects. The migration dynamics in these countries further exacerbate these challenges, requiring interpreters to speak foreign languages spoken by migrant workers, refugees, and asylum seekers.

3.2 Setting the Scene: Court Interpreting in Southern Africa

A crucial component of the legal systems in Zimbabwe, South Africa, Malawi, and Mozambique is courtroom interpretation, especially in light of the historical background of colonialism and the multilingual environment. Therefore, regardless of the linguistic background of those involved in the judicial process, the function of interpreters is essential in ensuring that justice is accessible to everyone. According to Svongoro, judicial interpreting has advanced significantly in Zimbabwe, especially in multilingual courtrooms where clear communication is crucial (Svongoro, 2024). The complexities of courtroom discourse necessitate a nuanced understanding of both language and legal processes. Court interpreters must, therefore, navigate these complexities to facilitate fair trials.

The significance of language rights is acknowledged in the 1996 and 2013 constitutions of South Africa and Zimbabwe, which have a direct bearing on judicial interpretation. For instance, Section 6 of the South African Constitution recognises eleven (now twelve) official languages and stipulates that everyone in the country must be able to communicate in their native tongue in court. Specifically, the Constitution of South Africa, Act 108 of 1996 at s35(3)(k) stipulates that 'every accused person has a right to a fair trial, which includes the right to be tried in a language that the accused person understands or, if that is not practicable, to have the proceedings interpreted in that language' (Moeketsi & Mollema, 2006:76). All these constitutional safeguards in Zimbabwe and South Africa's constitutions, for example, are essential for guaranteeing that those who do not speak the court's language can comprehend and take part in court proceedings (Quinot, 2024). The Promotion of Access to Justice Act in South Africa further emphasises the need for interpreters in court, stipulating that courts must provide interpreting services to ensure fair trial rights for all individuals, regardless of their language proficiency (Masiangoako, 2019).

The South African Courts Act, which describes the duties of court interpreters, is one of the other legal frameworks that regulate court interpreting in South Africa. During court hearings, interpreters are supposed to translate spoken language accurately and impartially in order to facilitate communication between the legal system and non-native English speakers (Kengni & Nkosi, 2023; Ndlovu, 2023b). This legislative requirement emphasises how important interpreters are to maintaining the values of justice and equity in the courtroom. However, despite the aforementioned constitutional and legal frameworks on language rights and the provision of court interpreting services, access to justice remains an unresolved issue because the legal systems of South Africa and Zimbabwe are based on the languages of the former colonisers (i.e., English for Zimbabwe and English/Afrikaans for South Africa).

The literature on court interpreting in Malawi indicates that in Malawi's legal system English is used as the language of legal proceedings and records (Kishindo, 2001; Nyirenda, 2014). However, in cases where the plaintiffs/defendants do not speak English, interpreters are provided. While the justice system makes provision for interpretation services for citizens who cannot speak English, there are two factors which militate against this state of affairs. First, Malawi is a highly non-literate country with an estimated non-literacy rate of 48 per cent (Kishindo, 2008).

Secondly, the majority of Malawi's population, including those who do not speak English, faces difficulties in communication due to the language barrier. Interpreters are needed to facilitate communication between courts and limited English proficient individuals. However, in Malawi, court interpreters are often poorly trained, under-resourced, and unavailable, leading to trial postponements. Research highlights the importance of well-trained and equipped interpreters in legal settings, as they not only translate words but also preserve the essence and nuances of the original message, which is crucial in high-stakes legal situations (Barak, 2021; Hale, 2021).

In Malawi, the laws governing courtroom interpretation are gradually evolving. Although standards are in place, they may not always be applied consistently. Since many interpreters might not be sufficiently prepared for the difficulties of legal interpreting, the absence of official training programmes for interpreters makes matters more difficult (Chawinga et al., 2019; Kondowe, 2022). This gap in training can lead to variations in the quality of interpreting services, ultimately affecting the judicial process.

Similar to the situations in Zimbabwe, South Africa, and Malawi, Mozambique is also a country which is characterised by a rich tapestry of over forty languages, including Portuguese, the official language, and various indigenous languages such as Makhuwa, Changana, Nyanja, Ndau, Sena, Chwabo, Tsonga and Tswa, Makhuwa, Sena, and Tsonga (Pereira, 2023). In order to promote communication between the court and others who might not speak Portuguese well, this language diversity calls for efficient interpreting services. In addition to translating words, interpreters also help close legal and cultural divides so that all parties can fully engage in the legal process and comprehend the proceedings (Hale, 2021; Pereira, 2023).

Despite ongoing difficulties related to its multilingual context, Mozambique's legal system offers a basis for judicial interpretation. The right to a fair trial, which includes the right to comprehend the proceedings, is guaranteed under the Mozambican Constitution. Article 62 (1) of the Constitution of the Republic of Mozambique stipulates that 'The State shall guarantee that citizens have access to the courts and that persons charged with a crime have the right to defence and the right to legal assistance and aid' (Constitution of the Republic of Mozambique, 2004:18). This provision clearly indicates that the Mozambican Constitution guarantees citizens the right to interpretation services and legal aid. However, the legal system, a blend of customary practices and civil law traditions, can be challenging to interpret due to the complexity of legal ideas and cultural nuances. This highlights the need for interpreters to possess a comprehensive understanding of legal jargon and language proficiency, as recommended by Ngubeni for South Africa, which also faces similar challenges (Ngubeni, 2023).

In the context of the issues raised earlier regarding language rights, the need for interpretation services and enhanced access to justice, this section, therefore, explores the legal framework governing courtroom interpreting in the aforementioned countries, the challenges faced by interpreters, the role of interpreters in ensuring justice, and the implications of language access in legal proceedings.

3.3 Court Interpreters' Role in the Judicial Process

Court interpreters are crucial intermediaries between the judiciary and litigants who do not know the court's official languages, such as English, Afrikaans, and Portuguese, which are used in Zimbabwe, South Africa, Malawi, and Mozambique. Their function goes beyond simple translation; they actively participate in the dynamics of the courtroom and use their interpretations to impact the proceedings.

As revealed in the literature on legal interpreting from Southern Africa, court interpreters serve as essential intermediaries between the judiciary and litigants who are unfamiliar with the court's official languages, such as English, Afrikaans, and Portuguese (Lebese, 2013; Ngubeni, 2023; Svongoro & Kondowe, 2024). This observation confirms Hale's research about Australian courtrooms. Hale emphasises that interpreters are not passive actors; rather, they are essential in influencing the discourses in the courtroom and, ultimately, the outcome of cases (Hale, 2021). This assertion is supported by Yi, who highlights the challenges interpreters face in maintaining accuracy and pragmalinguistic fidelity in their interpretations, particularly in high-stakes environments like courtrooms (Yi, 2023). However, when one considers the literature on the role of court interpreters in Zimbabwe, South Africa, Malawi, and Mozambique, issues related to court interpreters' role perception, and support given to court interpreters so that they can perform that duties optimally appear in the literature frequently (Lebese, 2013; Ngubeni, 2023; Svongoro & Kondowe, 2024). Because of the lack of clarity on the court interpreters' role, Lebese reports that in South Africa, such court interpreters find themselves performing tasks that are outside their scope of duties, for example, acting as magistrates (Lebese, 2013).

Court interpreters are essential to making sure that justice is carried out in South African courts. By enabling communication between parties who speak different languages, interpreters support, the Constitution's guarantee of a fair trial. In criminal trials for example, where misunderstandings which emerge from language issues can result in erroneous convictions or acquittals, court interpreters play a crucial role (Lebese, 2013; Ngubeni, 2023). Moreover, interpreters contribute to the overall integrity of the judicial process by ensuring that all parties can fully understand the proceedings and present their cases effectively.

Still on South Africa, the role of court interpreters is equally significant in civil cases. Court interpreters assist in mediating disputes, ensuring that all parties can articulate their positions and understand the implications of legal decisions (Maphosa & Nhlapo, 2020). This function is particularly important in cases involving vulnerable populations, such as migrant workers, asylum seekers and refugees, or individuals from marginalised communities, who may already face systemic barriers to accessing justice (Maphosa & Nhlapo, 2020). Researchers in the South African jurisdiction also view court interpreters in South Africa's justice system as cultural brokers, providing context and nuance that may not be captured in direct translations. This cultural understanding can enhance the accuracy of interpretations and contribute to a more equitable legal process (Moeketsi, 1999a, 1999b; Moeketsi & Wallmach, 2005). As such, the role of interpreters extends beyond mere translation; they are integral to the functioning of a just legal system.

Similar functions to those reported for court interpreters in South Africa and Zimbabwe are depicted in the literature on the function of court interpreters in Malawi. In Malawian courtrooms, court interpreters are essential agents of communication that guarantee all parties understand the proceedings. They are not spectators; their interpretations have a big impact on the outcome of cases. The fact that interpreters have to deal with intricate legal jargon, technical terms, and cultural nuances, which can compromise the precision of their interpretations, emphasises their active role (Barak, 2021). The interpreter's performance is critical, as inaccuracies can lead to misunderstandings that may compromise the fairness of the trial.

However, in the jurisdictions of the countries under review, research reports that the lack of legal terminology in many languages poses a significant challenge to accurate interpretation, particularly in cases where an accused's freedom, rights, or even their good name is at stake (Moeketsi & Mollema, 2006; Svongoro & Wallmach, 2022; Ngubeni, 2023). As a result, court interpreters in these jurisdictions are often accused of incompetent interpreting and bad practices which adversely affects access to justice (Moeketsi & Mollema, 2006; Docrat, 2022)

3.4 Challenges Faced by Court Interpreters

The literature reviewed on legal interpreting in the selected Southern African countries also reveals that despite the critical role they play, courtroom interpreters in Zimbabwe, South Africa, Malawi, and Mozambique encounter numerous challenges (Kishindo, 2008; Lebese, 2013; Usadalo & Kotzé, 2015; Matende et al., 2022a & 2022b). These include the intricacies of legal language, cultural nuances, the work environment, and the psychological pressure of real-time interpretation.

Usadolo and Kotzé (2015) also report about foreign language court interpreters in South Africa. They document the challenges faced by court interpreters in cross-border languages, such as Chisena and Afrikaans, when interpreting between neighbouring countries. The study suggests that interpreters may not be adequately informed about sociocultural issues and the different orthographies used for the languages, raising the need for court interpreters to be well-informed about relevant circumstances of each case and conduct pre-trial interviews to mitigate these challenges (Usadalo & Kotzé, 2015). Furthermore, the sociopolitical context in the four countries as explored by Verheul complicates the atmosphere in which interpreters operate, often leading to additional stressors that can affect their performance (Verheul, 2020, Matende et al., 2022a).

In all the four countries, court interpreters face the challenge related to the need for high levels of accuracy and the pressure of working in high-stakes environments (Matende et al., 2022a). However, the intricacies of legal language, combined with the sociocultural contexts of the parties involved, can lead to pragmatic challenges in interpretation (Yi, 2023). Furthermore, interpreters often face the dilemma of balancing fidelity to the source language with the need to convey meaning in a culturally appropriate manner (Moeketsi,

1999a; Moeketsi & Wallmach, 2005). This balancing act is crucial, as misinterpretations can have serious legal ramifications.

In South Africa, for example, despite the robust legal framework governing court interpreting, the court interpreting profession in South Africa still faces the shortage of qualified interpreters, particularly in rural areas where access to legal services is limited and in cases requiring foreign language interpreters (Usadolo, 2010). This shortage can lead to delays in court proceedings and may compromise the quality of interpretation, ultimately affecting the outcomes of cases. Furthermore, interpreters often work under high-pressure conditions, which can lead to stress and burnout, impacting their performance (Matende et al., 2022a).

Another challenge revealed in the literature about South Africa but also applies to Zimbabwe, Malawi, and Mozambique is the lack of standardised training and certification for interpreters. While some interpreters may possess linguistic skills, they may lack the specialised training required to navigate the complexities of legal terminology and courtroom procedures (Ngubeni, 2023). This gap in training can result in misinterpretations that could have serious implications for the parties involved in legal proceedings.

Additionally, the sociopolitical context of South Africa, characterised by historical injustices of apartheid and ongoing inequalities, can influence the dynamics of courtroom interpreting. Interpreters may encounter biases or prejudices from legal professionals or court officials, which can hinder their ability to perform their duties effectively. This environment necessitates a greater awareness of the social implications of interpreting work and the need for interpreters to advocate for their rights and the rights of those they serve. Docrat and de Vries (2022) also report about the continued marginalisation and politicisation of the African languages in the South African legal system occurring under the guise of transformation, which may also pose challenges for court interpreters who will have to work in such an environment.

Still on the sociopolitical environment in which court interpreters perform their duties, the literature reviewed reveals that the court interpreting profession in Southern Africa is influenced by linguistic diversity, cultural practices, socio-economic, and political factors. In Zimbabwe, for example, the available literature reports that political tensions, judicial corruption, and economic instability can create mistrust and fear, affecting individuals' willingness to engage with the legal system (Verheul, 2020). Referring to the malpractices and political interference in judicial practices at Rotten Row Magistrates' Courts in Zimbabwe, Verheul says, 'Rotten Row is Rotten to the Core' (Verheul, 2020: 9). Interpreters must, therefore, be aware of these dynamics to navigate their roles effectively. In Malawi, cultural competency is crucial for accurate interpretations

(Kishindo, 2008), while in Mozambique, cultural practices and beliefs can influence legal perceptions and interactions. Culturally competent interpreters can handle legal terminology and ensure each party feels valued and understood during legal proceedings. A similar situation is also reported in the Kenyan jurisdiction (O'Nyangeri, Habwe, & Omboga, 2022).

The literature on court interpreting in Mozambique also reveals multiple challenges. Most of the challenges reported can impact the quality of interpreting services provided in courts of law. As reported about South Africa, one significant challenge about court interpreting in Mozambique is the lack of standardised training programmes for interpreters, which leads to varying levels of proficiency and understanding of legal concepts among practitioners. This inconsistency can result in misinterpretations that affect the outcomes of legal proceedings. Moreover, the cultural context in which legal terms are used can differ significantly between languages, making it essential for interpreters to navigate these differences skilfully (Kishindo, 2008; Usadolo, 2010; Usadalo & Kotzé, 2015; Matende et al., 2022a).

Another challenge common in Mozambique is the limited availability of resources, including access to legal dictionaries and glossaries in indigenous languages. This scarcity can hinder interpreters' ability to provide accurate translations, particularly in complex legal cases where precise terminology is crucial. Additionally, the increasing use of technology in legal proceedings, accelerated by the COVID-19 pandemic, introduced new dynamics in interpreting, such as remote interpreting, which may not always be conducive to effective communication (Pereira, 2023).

Finally, the literature highlights the ethical challenges faced by court interpreters globally, including confidentiality, impartiality, and accuracy, and the need for professional standards to ensure justice, particularly in Zimbabwe, where the legal system is still developing (Matende et al., 2022a). In Malawi, ethical considerations are crucial, as interpreters are bound by a code of ethics emphasising confidentiality, impartiality, and accuracy (Kishindo, 2008; Nyirenda, 2014). However, high-stakes environments can lead to ethical dilemmas, especially when interpreting statements that may be prejudicial or inflammatory. Thus, how court interpreters navigate these ethical challenges is essential for maintaining the integrity of the judicial process.

3.5 The Impact of Interpreting Innovations and Technology on Court Interpreting

In line with the provisions of South Africa's Constitution which guarantees the right to be tried in a language one understands or have proceedings interpreted in that language if possible, South Africa introduced an innovative programme aimed to enhance the quality of interpretation services so as to ensure increased access to justice for those individuals court interpreters mediate. Moeketsi and Mollema (2006) report about the concept of Perfect Interpreting Practice (PIP) which was developed in South Africa with the aim of addressing the poor quality of interpreting common in South Africa's courts and transforming the service and fostering a culture of quality, accountability, and continuous improvement.

The integration of technology into the judicial process has transformed court interpreting in Zimbabwe, Malawi, and Mozambique. In Zimbabwe, for example, the adoption of digital platforms, such as the Integrated Electronic Case Management System (IECMS), aims to streamline court operations and improve access to justice (Poshai & Vyas-Doorgapersad, 2023). In Malawi, Chawinga et al. (2019) also report about how the move towards e-judicial services will impact on justice delivery in Malawi. However, the reliance on technology also presents challenges, particularly in ensuring that interpreters can effectively communicate in virtual settings. The technology-related challenges reported about court interpreters in Zimbabwe are similar to those reported by Yi's research on remote interpreting in Chinese courtrooms. Yi's study highlights the difficulties interpreters face in maintaining accuracy and clarity when working through video conferencing tools, which have become increasingly common since the outbreak of the COVID-19 pandemic (Yi, 2023).

Although the previous paragraph indicates that southern African countries are making strides in transforming court interpreting through technology integration, advancements in remote (videoconferencing) interpreting (RI) are still limited. RI has grown significantly in Europe and the Americas, with large institutions like the United Nations and the European Union using it for simultaneous interpreting (Gloria, 2018). The International Association of Conference Interpreters (AIIC) published guidelines on distant interpreting after the COVID-19 pandemic. However, remote work adds cognitive loads and communication challenges, such as screen fatigue, increased stress, limited contextual information, noise exposure, and difficulties in rota teamwork (Liu, 2022). These issues are often not included in existing interpreting curricula, and research on these areas is limited. Additionally, many trainers may not have worked on RI platforms themselves, making it challenging to train the next generation of interpreters.

Apart from the aforementioned, the lack of literature on computer-assisted interpretation (CAI) in Southern Africa indicates a lack of adoption of this technology. CAI aims to improve interpreters' productivity through tools like terminology management solutions, notetaking applications, and voice-to-text devices. Terminology management tools are the most widely used CAI solutions, with InterpretBank being a popular example. However, existing CAI terminology tools are platform-dependent, time-consuming, and require training and practice (Claudio, 2018; Gloria, 2018). Research on the role of CAI tools for interpretation is limited, but some studies suggest that under specific circumstances, they may improve booth quality and reduce cognitive load during simultaneous interpreting.

Looking ahead, artificial intelligence (AI) is gaining momentum in interpreting, with the goal of replacing human interpreters with machines. Current AI solutions include automatic speech recognition, machine translation, and speech-to-text synthesis (Claudio, 2018; Gloria, 2018; Liu, 2022). However, although these systems are yet to be tried in the southern African countries reviewed in this section, these systems have struggled to achieve quality and usability in real scenarios where they are under trials. The AIIC in the UK and Ireland, for example, organised online events on AI and interpreting, presenting scenarios where machine interpreting solutions could be applied. These solutions could be particularly useful in public service interpreting settings, where interpreters face challenges like reduced demand, budget constraints, and English as the default language.

3.6 Multilingualism and Its Implications for Access to Justice

Zimbabwe's linguistic diversity necessitates a robust framework for court interpreting. The country's official languages include English, Shona, and IsiNdebele, among others, which complicate the legal landscape. While Zimbabwe recognises sixteen official languages, Zimbabwe's language of record policy contradicts this recognition. In courts of law, English is the language used for proceedings and records, including during police-suspect /witness interviews at police stations. This language of record policy is seen as having serious implications for access to justice by the majority of Zimbabweans who speak indigenous languages. Speakers of indigenous languages continue to encounter injustices and prejudices while recording witness accounts at police stations (Muza, 2008).

The implications of multilingualism and language access in legal proceedings are far more profound in South Africa than in Zimbabwe and Malawi. In South Africa, where many individuals may not speak English or Afrikaans, the dominant languages of the legal system, language barriers can significantly hinder access to justice (van Niekerk, 2015; Namakula, 2023). The inability to understand legal proceedings can lead to feelings of alienation and distrust in the judicial system, further perpetuating social inequalities (Muza, 2008).

Another concern about South Africa's justice system which poses challenges on the provision of interpreting services is South Africa's language of record policy brought to light by studies conducted in South African courtrooms and police stations (van Niekerk, 2015; Docrat & Kaschula, 2024). These researchers concur that, even though the nation's English-only language of record policy has been a part of the South African legal system since 2017, it still prevents speakers of other languages from accessing the justice system fully as they have to participate in the justice system through an intermediary.

Moreover, language access issues can have tangible consequences for the outcomes of legal cases. Research has shown that individuals who do not have access to competent interpreting services are more likely to experience negative legal outcomes, including longer sentences or unfavourable rulings (Svongoro & Kadenge, 2015). This reality underscores the urgent need for systemic reforms to improve language access in South African courts. As suggested by Svongoro, justice systems in Africa need to strive for the provision of interpreters who are not only linguistically proficient but also culturally competent (Svongoro, 2024). This cultural awareness is crucial for interpreters to accurately convey the intent and nuances of the original statements made in court.

To address these challenges, stakeholders must advocate for increased funding and resources to support the training and recruitment of qualified interpreters (Maphosa & Nhlapo, 2020). Additionally, the establishment of standardised training programmes and certification processes can enhance interpreters' skills in legal language and courtroom dynamics. Raising awareness about language access is crucial for legal professionals and court officials. Emphasising interpreters' value and the impact of language barriers on justice can create a more inclusive legal environment (Usadalo & Kotzé, 2015; Docrat, 2022).

As for Malawi, the quality of court interpreting directly impacts the access to justice for individuals who do not speak Portuguese. When interpreters are not adequately trained or when interpreting services are unavailable, individuals may struggle to understand the legal proceedings, leading to potential miscarriages of justice. Ensuring that all parties have access to competent interpreting services is essential for upholding the principles of fairness and equality in the legal system (Kishindo, 2008). Legal aid organisations and advocacy groups can play a crucial role in raising awareness about the importance of interpreting services and advocating for policy changes that support their implementation.

3.7 Challenges in the Training for Interpreters

The training of courtroom interpreters is essential for enhancing the quality of interpreting services in all legal settings. In Zimbabwe, literature reveals that there are still gaps in the training and employment requirements for court interpreters. The current in-service training programme for court interpreters does not address the unique challenges posed by the legal environment, as highlighted in prior studies (Svongoro & Kadenge, 2015; Svongoro, 2024). Research also advocates for the reconceptualisation of the interpreter's role to include a focus on sociocultural dynamics could also be relevant for the Zimbabwean context (Ndlovu, 2023b; Svongoro & Kondowe, 2024). Rather than focusing on language skills only, effective training should also encompass an understanding of legal terminology, courtroom procedures, and ethical considerations.

Similar to the Zimbabwean situation, the literature on Mozambique also highlights the need for comprehensive training and professional development programmes to address the challenges faced by court interpreters, focusing on enhancing linguistic skills, legal knowledge, and cultural awareness through workshops, seminars, and mentorship opportunities (Pereira, 2023). Furthermore, collaboration with legal institutions and universities could facilitate the development of standardised curricula that address the specific needs of court interpreters in Mozambique.

3.8 Future Directions for Courtroom Interpreting in Southern African Courtrooms

Looking ahead, the future of court interpreting in southern African countries discussed in this section will likely be shaped by ongoing technological advancements, the fast-evolving migration trends, and the linguistic and legal landscape in the countries. The integration of blockchain technology used in other parts of the world, as discussed by Kumar, Kumar, and Joshi (2023), presents opportunities for enhancing transparency and efficiency in court operations, which could also benefit interpreting practices (Kumar, Kumar, & Joshi, 2023). However, it is crucial to ensure that these technological innovations do not compromise the quality of interpreting services.

Looking at Malawi, for example, the future of court interpreting will likely be shaped by ongoing reforms in the legal system and advancements in technology. There is a growing recognition of the need for standardised training programmes for interpreters to enhance their skills and ensure consistent quality across the board (Chawinga et al., 2019; Kondowe, 2022). Additionally, as the legal landscape continues to evolve, interpreters will need to adapt to new challenges and opportunities presented by technological advancements.

For Mozambique, there are several key areas for development in court interpreting. First, increasing collaboration between legal institutions, interpreter training organisations, and community stakeholders can foster a more integrated approach to interpreting services. Furthermore, it will be crucial to use technology to improve interpreting procedures while making sure interpreters are properly trained in its use in order to adjust to the changing legal environment. Finally, ongoing research into the effectiveness of interpreting services and their impact on legal outcomes will be critical for informing future policies and practices.

3.9 Conclusion

The literature reviewed in this section has shown that court interpreting is a multifaceted field that requires a deep understanding of language, culture, and the legal system. This section has shown that the challenges faced by interpreters are significant, yet their role is indispensable in ensuring that justice is accessible to all (Ndlovu, 2023b). In addition, this section has also shown that as the judicial landscape continues to evolve, ongoing training, ethical considerations, and the integration of technology will be vital in enhancing the effectiveness of court interpreting in all the countries discussed in this section.

Concerning South Africa, for example, this section has shown that court interpreting is a vital aspect of the legal system that directly impacts the administration of justice. The legal framework provides a foundation for language rights, yet significant challenges remain in ensuring effective interpretation services (Usadalo & Kotzé, 2015; Docrat, 2022). South Africa must prioritise language access in legal proceedings, invest in interpreter training, advocate for systemic reforms, and foster inclusivity within the legal system to address its complex linguistic landscape and the legacy of apartheid, thereby achieving true justice for all citizens.

Regarding Malawi, this section has shown that court interpreting is a multifaceted and dynamic field that is essential to guaranteeing that everyone, regardless of language proficiency, has access to justice (Kishindo, 2008). Interpreters in Malawi face ongoing challenges due to evolving legal and technological landscapes. Despite these challenges, their role remains crucial in fostering understanding and access to justice within the courtroom, emphasising the need for ongoing training and support.

In Mozambique, judicial interpretation is a complex matter that necessitates careful evaluation of language, cultural, and legal aspects (Pereira, 2023). The literature on court interpreting in Mozambique highlights the need for comprehensive training, technology integration, and cultural competence. Addressing these issues can improve access to justice and ensure a just legal system. The future of court interpreting in Mozambique will be shaped by ongoing research and language rights advocacy.

In the following section issues pertaining to police interviewing techniques will be critiqued.

4 An Overview of the Challenges in Police Investigative Interviewing in Multilingual Southern Africa

4.1 Introduction

The need to ensure that fair justice is delivered in multilingual and multicultural contexts such as southern Africa has been a major challenge whereby selective and discriminating language policies adopted by the countries concerned are to blame for pushing potential stakeholders, particularly vulnerable suspects, to risk unfair imprisonment or other forms of penalties. Despite the discipline of forensic linguistics being particularly new to Africa and to southern Africa in particular, there has been growing research conducted by emerging scholars in the field. These young academics have brought to light the seriousness of the problems and the challenges raised by the adoption of language policies that hinder fair delivery of justice for speakers of languages other than those selected for the justice system.

Bearing in mind that overall, in the lawyers' and police officers' viewpoint, multilingualism is the major source of communication difficulties and hence the chaos occasionally facing legal proceedings, this section attempts to explore the origins of police interviewing in southern Africa and also problematises the impact caused by the adoption and use of non-inclusive language policies on speakers of minority or non-official languages, and also attempts to raise awareness about the role played by the attitudes police officers adopt when dealing with the aforesaid people. Qualitative data from experiences from a few southern African countries will be used to demonstrate why African multilingualism should halt from being viewed as a curse put on linguistically disadvantaged people in police investigative interviewing.

As stated in Section 1, the history of the forensic discipline in southern Africa is very recent, and it was probably formally started with the work by Moeketsi (1999a & 1999b). In this work, although the focus was not exactly on police interviewing *strictu sensu*, she raised the problem on the role of interpreters in multilingual South Africa, a country with eleven official languages at that time [now with twelve official languages after the South African sign language was added], in which nine of these languages are African languages. Despite this, and likewise in other southern African countries, only two languages are used in the justice system, thus demanding the use of professional interpreters as indicated in the previous section. More recently, other countries in the region, such as Mozambique, Zimbabwe, and Malawi also started their engagement in the field of forensic linguistics, despite not particularly focusing in police investigative interviewing.

The African continent, particularly in its sub-Saharan area, is widely known for its multilingualism and multiculturalism shared by its various countries.

This heritage, which has been alive for centuries, is viewed by linguists, anthropologists, sociologists, and scholars of the various fields of knowledge in the social sciences and humanities as a precious source of primary data for their research due to its uniqueness. Nonetheless, the fact that most sub-Saharan African countries have in general inherited a language of the former colonial power, a language which is not shared by the majority who are speakers of an African language as their mother tongues, poses a huge challenge particularly when it comes to fair delivery of justice.

Indeed, for years, sub-Saharan African people as a whole and southern African communities in particular have always had to carry their shoulders the burden of coping with an imposed language of the former colonial power, which is often alien to them. This language, which is a language of a minority elite, is eventually the sole official language and, therefore, the only language of the judicial system. In the particular case of former Portuguese colonies [and unlike in former British countries] and most certainly in former French colonies as Chimbutane (2016) indicates, the situation is even worse as communities had to live under the so-called *assimilationist* policy. This policy consisted of discouraging indigenous people from speaking their own mother tongues and also to abandon all of their cultural values and embrace the language and habits of the 'civilised' man. Under the aforementioned policy, Mozambicans in particular were therefore denied their culture and the right to speak their own languages which would then be labelled as the 'dogs' languages' or the 'languages of the uncivilized people'.

In most countries in sub-Saharan Africa, the prevailing state of affairs during the colonial times was then replicated after independence with a huge impact in the delivery of justice for the majority of vulnerable people for whom the sole official language was and still is alien to them. In former Portuguese colonies, the ruling regimes drafted Constitutions mostly based on the principles of the laws enforced in the European colonial power. In some cases, the language issue in the first Constitutions of these countries was left unspecified in what was known as avoidance of policy formulation in Bamgbose's (1991) terms or even as 'taboo' as Lopes (2004) argues. In Mozambique, for instance, despite the fact that neither the 1975 Constitution nor its revised version from 1978 made a statement on the language situation, the use of African languages in official settings was (and still is to some extent) implicitly forbidden.

As it is known, former British colonies in Africa have gone through a slightly different path as far as the language policy issue is concerned. Whereas in Portuguese-occupied territories the prevailing strategy was the aforesaid *assimilationist* policy, in British colonies indigenous languages were 'tolerated' to some reasonable degree, though their use would be very limited to their communities as no promotion would almost never occur at the official level. Nonetheless, since education is the key for development, most of these countries adopted some kind of mother tongue education before and after independence that enabled the development of the individual languages (Ghana, Sierra Leone, Zimbabwe, South Africa, just to mention a few). This relative language development, however, could not persuade the colonial authorities to accept their use in official context such as in the judicial system.

4.2 Language Policies and Fair Delivery of Justice

As mentioned before, the language policies adopted by most countries in the sub-Saharan Africa are very selective as to ensure fair delivery of justice, particularly for speakers of minority languages. This phenomenon seems to affect people in several ways in both former Portuguese and British colonies. Heydon and Mabasso conducted research in Maputo, the capital city of Mozambique, which aimed at ascertaining how domestic violence (DV) cases were reported by victims, mostly non-speakers of Portuguese, the official language and the language of the justice system. Domestic violence has been one of the major crime types that on-duty police officers are increasingly required to address in most police stations in Mozambique, particularly in the main cities such as the capital Maputo and its outskirts. In 2009 a Bill on DV was passed by the Mozambican Parliament, which explicitly aims at protecting women and girls [not men] from being assaulted by men (Act no. 29/2009).

Despite the aforementioned legal tool, language constraints still hinder victims' effort to implement their rights as the law is written in a language which is alien to them. There is indeed a potential for miscarriages of justice to occur in police interviews in Maputo due to the linguistic diversity of suspects and their lack of proficiency in Portuguese, the official language of Mozambique. It should therefore be borne in mind that '... lack of proficiency in a State's official language can prevent access to justice' (Gibbons, 2003a:211–221).

In Maputo, victims face language-related obstacles when making reports about domestic violence to a range of justice agencies. These are their ultimate refuge as they no longer rely on the police, mostly for being intolerant towards their language limitations. Lawyers and police officers view lack of knowledge of rights by DV victims not as a problem at all because, overall, they do not '... need to understand the law' (Heydon & Mabasso, 2018).

The earlier statement by a lawyer [they don't need to understand the judge] is a clear pointer that it is believed among that particular group of legal professionals that multilingualism as a social and cultural phenomenon is problematic and rather something to be ignored and that victims only need to hear what their legal representatives will tell them about the progress of their cases. Indeed, lawyers and legal professionals in general are known for their reluctance and keenness to defend the interests of their group at any cost. This could explain why, for instance, plain language movements across the world usually face opposition when approaching the judicial authorities to present proposals of simplified varieties of pieces of the legal language; such was the case of the simplified version of police cautions in Australia (Gibbons, 2001).

4.3 The Need for Interpreters

In Mozambique, for instance, where Portuguese is the only official language, very often police officers and judges are challenged by the need to comply with the legal provisions on language, on the one hand, and, on the other hand, the need to drive the case to a verdict particularly by obtaining a confession or a statement from the suspect/ defendant. Very often, these people do not speak the language of the justice system and are not proficient enough to face either an interrogation at a police station in a language that is alien to them.

As it has been suggested elsewhere, the judicial system faces a dilemma as a consequence of the single official language policy in multilingual countries, on the one hand, and the lack of police station and courtroom interpreters on the other hand. There are cases where despite a judge being a speaker of the defendants' language, in an attempt to comply with the legal provision on the matter, they would struggle to keep the conversation in the official language. Cases have been also reported (Mabasso, 2019) where the defendant understands the questions they were asked in the official language, but they prefer to present their side of the story in their mother tongue, the only code they can master with ease.

4.4 English as the Only Language of Record

This section is further supported by Section 2 of this Element, which deals with the issue of language of record in more detail. South Africa is another country where multilingualism has been seen as a challenge for the judicial system and fair justice delivery. Section 6 of the 1996 Country's Constitution states as follows on the language issue:

(1) The official languages of the Republic are Sepedi, Sesotho, Setswana, siSwati, Tshivenda, Xitsonga, Afrikaans, English, isiNdebele, isiXhosa and isiZulu.
(2) Recognising the historically diminished use and status of the indigenous languages of our people, the state must take practical and positive measures to elevate the status and advance the use of these languages.

At first sight both subsections (1) and (2) clearly provide a comprehensive type of language policy whereby the African languages are given prominence and it is here recognised the need for the rapid development of their status in order to be used alongside English and/or Afrikaans. Docrat and Kaschula (2019) and also De Vries and Docrat (2019) in their recent studies have problematised the language choice by the judicial authorities, in which English has been given greater prominence than the other ten official languages, despite the aforementioned constitutional provision.

The authors' major concern is related to the fact that a directive has been issued in which all South African High Courts should adopt English as the only language of record, despite the country's Constitution additionally acknowledging the other ten languages as official alongside English. All the eleven official languages (now twelve), according to the South African Constitution, should be treated equally in all public domains, including the judicial system. Moreover, selected university language policies, namely the University of Free State (UFS), University of Pretoria (UP), University of Cape Town (UCT), University of KwaZulu-Natal (UKZN), University of Stellenbosch, and Rhodes University, have been vastly critiqued as to how they fail to challenge the maintenance of the status quo as far as the language of court record is concerned (Docrat & Kaschula, 2019; Docrat et al., 2021).

Docrat and Kaschula (2019) indicate as the major ground for their argument the fact that South Africa's bilingualism and multilingualism are not being given their deserved relevance when it comes to determining the language of record. English remains the only language of record, and the other ten official languages are left behind. Unfortunately, as they put it, the aforementioned selected country universities, with UKZN as an exception, do not play their role to influence language of record policymakers to also include indigenous languages as languages or record. Furthermore, Docrat and Kaschula (2019) pointed out that university language policies are challenged to adopt policies that are reflective of the language demographics of the provinces where they are located and the broader demographics of South Africa.

Another key point raised by both authors is that law faculties and African Language Departments should collaborate in formulating courses that are of benefit to students in a professional context. In their view, this would persuade law makers to include skills in at least one African language as key requirement for legal professionals. The authors recommended that South African authorities consider collaboration with forensic linguists in order to advise the process of formulating sound policies where language rights of potential litigants would be safeguarded (Docrat & Kaschula, 2019).

Further north, and despite Ghana being a country outside the limits of the southern African region, it is also a multilingual country, with both societal and individual multilingualism also facing challenges when it comes to fair deliver of justice, according to a recent study by Ansah and Darko (2019). As for the language issue in the justice system, the country's 1992 Constitution, Article 19(2), states as follows:

A person charged with criminal offence shall

> (d) be informed immediately in a language that he understands, and in detail; of the nature of the offence charged;
> (h) be permitted to have, without payment by him, the assistance of an interpreter where he cannot understand the language use at the trial.

Similarly, to South Africa and apart from being the language of the court, English is also the language of record in Ghana. Most importantly, among the seventy-three indigenous languages out of eighty-one languages spoken in the country, nine are sponsored by the Government. Despite this, the hegemony enjoyed by English is undeniable, particularly in the justice system. In other words, and like in many other multilingual countries in Africa, the language of the former colonial power is still regarded as the most reliable to conduct court hearings and keep records.

4.5 Legal Interpreters as Gap Builders

Even if more inclusive language policies are to be approved in multilingual and multicultural southern Africa, and therefore their use in the judicial system, issues will still remain unresolved, namely the need to work out the necessary legal terminology in African languages on the one hand, and the need to make the message as much understandable as possible, on the other hand. This is in part because legal genres have always been known for their excessive use of tortuous syntax, very long sentences, circumlocutions, prepositional phrases, the use of Latinisms, and other forms of archaisms, in an effort to protect legal professionals and also as a manifest of its elitism and distance towards the general lay people (Bathia, 1994). This is the point where universities in which degrees in African languages and translation are offered are called upon to play their role by providing support in the development status of these languages.

Interpreters are viewed as the main stakeholders in the process of conveying communication in a judicial case, where one of the parties does not speak the language of the court. Indeed, the use of interpreters as gap builders has been gaining room over the few years in most multilingual countries in Africa. Most Constitutions and other legal tools provide guidelines on the use of interpreters where a witness, defendant, or plaintiff cannot speak the language of the court.

Whereas in some countries the side which pays the costs for the interpreting work is clearly indicated in the legal provision, in most other countries this is left unspecified, thus giving room for flexible interpretation.

In the aforementioned Ghanaian case, the country's Constitution in its article 19(2) clearly states that no charges should be held on to the person whose language is other than the court's language. This indicates that Government authorities will cover all costs regarding the interpreting service. Many would claim that it would be rather redundant for a legal provision to explicitly indicate that point; however, it should be recalled that, in most African countries, vagueness, or even arbitrariness in Bamgbose's (1991) terms, has always been a widespread technique adopted by a range of regimes, with a view at maintaining the status quo, that is, the hegemony of the language inherited from the former colonial power.

By acknowledging the use of twelve official languages, of which ten [including the recently promoted South African sign language] are of African origin, the South African Constitution recognises the right for nationals who speak each of the languages to use them in all official contexts, including in the judicial system. Research conducted by several scholars in South Africa such as Moeketsi (1999a, 1999b), Ralarala and Rodrigues (2019), Docrat and Kaschula (2019), De Vries and Docrat (2019), and Ralarala and Lesh (2022) demonstrate that, apart from the challenges faced with the quality in the interpreting task, the government authorities provide interpreters whenever deemed necessary.

In Mozambique, probably the only Portuguese-speaking country in which forensic linguistics and mostly particularly police interviewing have been experiencing some insightful developments, the Civil Process Code in its 2010 revised version made this point clear:

Article 139
(Courtroom Language)
1. Portuguese shall be the language for courtroom sessions.

Those who do not speak Portuguese and wish to be heard shall, however, [be permitted to do so] in a language other than Portuguese, provided that, if deemed necessary, a sworn interpreter is appointed to ensure communication.

While these amendments of Article 139 earlier made clear that interpreters were required whenever the witness did not speak Portuguese, it is important to note that this Article failed to specify who would pay for the interpreting service. In practice, the responsibility for paying for an interpreter lied entirely upon the individual who made the request.

However, in 2019, a new Penal Procedural Code was approved and new developments added information to the aforementioned Article, through Act no. 25/2019 of 26 September and Article 102(1)(2), which reads as follows:

Article 102

(Courtroom language and appointment of interpreters)
1. Portuguese shall be the language for procedural acts, both written and spoken, otherwise the act shall be deemed null.
2. In the event of a participant who is not competent enough in the official language, a professional interpreter shall be appointed with no charges held on to him, even when the person in charge of the procedural act or either party are speakers of that language.

Given that the 2019 code is a relatively new tool, and also taking into account the historical fact that enforcement of new laws in some developing countries can take time to be fully taken to the general public, and also bearing in mind the lack of professional interpreters, time will tell when this legal provision will see the light of the day.

Interpreters play a key role in conveying communication when speakers of languages other the official language have to speak before a police station or a court of law. Despite the fact that most Constitutions will recognise their role, the quality of their work is not assured by any legal provision, with the impact thereof. More precisely, the job of interpreters as gap fillers has been long critiqued for poor quality and lack of legally oriented training. Among those who critique their job most, judges are in the frontline, as pointed out by Docrat and Kaschula (2019) or even Heydon and Mabasso (2018).

However, the most concerning issue in the translation process is the use of ad hoc interpreters, who are mostly either on-duty police officers or particularly relatives of suspects. In court cases, this role is usually played by court assistants or clerks. In the case of suspects, and as Berk-Seligson (2009) puts it, there is a potential for police officers to obtain confessions through coercion, thus risking suspect's rights. Likewise, in court cases, interpreters are usually said to lack skills, and, therefore, their job is useless. When asked about the need for defendants to be informed about a case in a language they know better, lawyers say that their clients do not need to understand the police or the judge, as mentioned earlier.

4.6 Police Interviewing Practices

Overall, available research covering police investigative interviewing techniques in Africa as a whole and particularly in southern African countries seems to be very scarce, and most studies seem to be related to issues of police interpreting, as mentioned earlier in this section. However, it was possible to track a few publications which can be helpful to ascertain how police interviewing is conducted in some representative countries.

Before going through some of the available literature on the matter, it is worth recalling that most Southern African countries are former British colonies which are formally ruled by some form of common law system, combined with other systems, except Mozambique and Angola, two former Portuguese colonies, which are ruled by the civil law system inherited from Portugal. For instance, South Africa follows a hybrid of Roman Dutch civilian law, English common law, customary law, and religious personal law; in Zimbabwe, the legal system consists of the common law legislation case law (precedent) and customary law; Botswana is known for its dual legal system, whereby Roman Dutch law exists side by side with customary law; Zambia's judicial system is based on English common law and customary law; Malawi's legal system is based on English law, which was modified in 1969; and Tanzania follows a common law system. In the case of Mozambique, despite customary law not formally stated as a legal system, its practices are widespread in police interviewing cases as Mabasso (2019) has pointed out.

Noteworthy is that, even countries that have not clearly indicated in their Constitutions that customary law methods can also be adopted by police as part of the legal system, the use of traditional tactics to interview suspects of certain crimes is likely to occur, and Malawi, Mozambique, and Angola are such examples. Clearly, this will impact the way police officers interview suspects.

Indeed, one of the most recent studies covering eleven sub-Saharan African nations was conducted by Donovan and Perez (2024). Although this study did not focus on southern African countries themselves, it managed to include a few such as Botswana, Malawi, Namibia, and South Africa, and common features could be drawn when it comes to police interviewing methods. In their study, Donovan and Perez indicated that, in their research countries, commonly used techniques are mostly based on 'expertise' shared by most experienced or senior police officers who have the rather challenging task of training their fellow colleagues to conduct reliable interviews with suspects. The use of strategies based on non-scientific methods is said to be behind the false confessions that have been reported by a few scholars, most probably due to the use of coercive methods.

However, an important step taken in southern African policing to address numerous issues related to police interviewing was the establishment of the Southern African Police Chiefs Cooperation Organisation (SARPCCO) in 1985. As a result, a Code of Conduct with thirteen articles was produced in 2011, with a view to promote, among other issues, Respect for Human Rights;

Non-discrimination; and for protection against Use of Force; Torture or other Cruel, Inhuman and Degrading Treatment or Punishment; Respect for the Rule of Law and Code of Conduct, and other measures to protect peoples' rights (Dissel & Frank, 2012). Notwithstanding the aforementioned, individual countries in southern Africa seem to adopt these principles differently. Experiences from a few Southern African countries in police interviewing are presented next.

4.6.1 Mozambique

Mozambique is one of the SARPCCO members which have largely been affected by a sole official language policy in a multilingual context, but the lack of a locally produced police interviewing protocol or formally defined police interviewing techniques has been a cause for concern. A study by Mabasso (2019) demonstrated that Master course students at the country's only police college known as ACIPOL (Academia de Ciências Policiais), who were mostly senior detectives working for the various police branches including criminal investigation, when asked about what technique or model they adopted when interviewing suspects, more specifically between a more coercive method such as the Reid Technique or PEACE Model, their response was to keep themselves silent. Their silence meant that they had never heard of anything about these two techniques. The meaning of each letter for the PEACE Model is as follows: P = Planning and Preparation; E = Engage and Explain; A = Account, clarification and challenge; C = Closure; and E = Evaluation. This model emerged in the 1990s in the UK as a response to a series of miscarriages of justice in cases such as the Birmingham Six (1974), the Guilford Four (1975), and the Manguire Seven (1976) (Mulayim et al., 2015). Today, in many first world countries, situations in which the police act on the presumption that the suspect is guilty are no longer justified. This model is based on the spirit that the truth must be found, no matter what (Mulayim et al., 2015). Cognitive interviewing, on the other hand, is divided into the following main steps: (i) Reporting All the Facts (everything you can remember); (ii) Reporting the Facts in Reverse Order (telling the facts in various chronological orders); (iii) Change Perspective (listen to the story from the perspective of a third person); and (iv) Reintegrate the Context (recall the physical environment surrounding the incident).

The Reid Technique, on the other hand, was developed in the United States, and its main aim is to train the police in persuading suspects to confess to the crimes they are accused of (Mulayim et al., 2015). The technique is characterised by two main approaches, namely maximisation, which includes intimidation and exaggeration about the seriousness of the crime and the charge. In the absence of a police interviewing guideline in Mozambique, and taking into account police interviewing practices so far reported across the country, it would be reasonable to believe that the Reid Technique is much closer to the practice adopted in Mozambique (Mabasso, 2019).

It would fair to believe that the use of customary law methods in Mozambique, a country ruled by the inquisitorial system, is a widespread practice, and this goes in line with some of the Reid Technique principles, particularly in cases where the police need to safeguard its legitimacy and authority before suspects. Of course, confusion and arbitrariness are likely to emerge as a result of attempting to enforce the law and, at the same time, adopt traditionally based means of delivering social justice (see Heydon & Mabasso, 2024). Requirements to become a police officer are limited to basic requirements such as having successfully completed grade 10 and then undertaking a basic police course (see Mabasso, 2019). Although ACIPOL has been providing training in criminal investigation at postgraduate levels, the majority of police officers who have the task of interviewing suspects still rely upon the basic skills learned during their training.

4.6.2 South Africa

South Africa adopted its first police Code of Conduct in 1997 as a result of reforms following the fall of the Apartheid regime, and an update took place in 2012 as a result of the various recommendations such as from SAPCCO. Most publications on the South African police interviewing context seem to be related to interpreting issues in police interviewing (see De Vries & Docrat, 2019; Ralarala & Rodrigues, 2019; Ralarala & Lesh, 2022). Nonetheless, the kinds of challenges facing the interviewing process in multilingual South Africa seem to be the same as in the previous case of Mozambique, despite the fact that South Africa has a more inclusive language policy, as mentioned earlier.

One of the indications for the need to enhance best interviewing practices by the police can be found in Hanekom (2021), in which she raises awareness on the need for South African authorities to adopt either the PEACE Model or the Reid Technique but taking into account necessary adaptations to the intercultural context. She argues for the need for the identification and adaptation to intercultural communication elements in investigative interviewing contexts, given that communication and culture should not be separated. Indeed, this is a more exploratory study which suggests how police interviewing should account for intercultural issues.

As far as training is concerned, Babili (2024) expressed his concern because the so-called police constables [the name given to uniformed police in the South African Police Service (SAPS)], who are mainly native speakers of other languages other than English, are hired to join the SAPS. These officers are hired on the basis of the following requirements: successful physical and a medical examination; no criminal background; and no body tattoos; matriculation certificates with a pass mark threshold of 30 per cent in English as a second language (2024). These are the police officers who conduct interviews in the various criminal cases, whose statements are used by courts as evidence.

4.6.3 Tanzania

Regarding Tanzania, a recent reference found which is related to police interviewing was from Ngogo (2025), who discussed the application of Information and Communication Technology (ICT) in police interviewing. One important thing to note is that the use of ICT in police interviewing aims at protecting peoples' rights against self-incrimination and unfair verbal interviews by the police that could lead to unfair suspects' conviction. Tanzania is one of the few countries in the region that have made an amendment to their Criminal Procedure Act through section 57(5)-(7), aimed at introducing the application of audio- and video-recording devices during the recording of the police interview with suspects, though this still has not come into effect (2025).

Another important aspect with the ICT implementation in police interviewing is to ensure that suspects' rights are fully assured, more specifically the right to remain silent and the right to be assisted by a lawyer and also to prevent false confessions to occur.

4.6.4 Zimbabwe

In Zimbabwe, an Investigation Procedure Manual dated 2016 establishes the guidelines that police officers should comply with when interviewing both complainants and suspects.[1] As for the interview and suspects with suspects, which interest most for this section, the Manual establishes that the suspect must be cautioned before being asked if he/she wishes to make any statement that would add value to their defence. The caution is stated in the same form as in most Western countries, such as the police cautions in Australia and England and Wales, but one important aspect is that the suspect is asked if they wish to say anything in their defence and, if the answer is 'no', then this should be recorded in the suspect's form.

Zimbabwe is also known for also being ruled by strong traditional leadership system which plays a role in the country's policing, especially in the

---

[1] https://lsu.ac.zw/public/assets/documents/Investigation_Procedure_Manual.pdf [access on 1 February 2025].

communities. These leaders, according to Zikhali (2019), '(...) derive their powers and roles from customary laws, culturally inherited values that are complemented by the Zimbabwean current legislation' (Zikhali, 2019:111). As a result, traditional leaders are empowered by the Zimbabwean legislation to preside over customary court trials where they enforce law according to local values and customs (Zikhali, 2019:111). This seems to be a good example for countries in the region, such as Angola and Mozambique, which still have not overtly adopted customary law practices in their legal system, despite the fact that police officers adopt them when interviewing suspects.

4.7 An Approach to the Méndez Principles

A major step has been taken by Southern African police authorities through the Southern African Regional Police Commissioners Cooperation Organisation (SARPCCO), in collaboration with the African Commission on Human and Peoples' Rights (ACHPR) and its Committee for the Prevention of Torture in Africa (CPTA), when they met last 1–2 July 2024, in Johannesburg, South Africa, with a view at promoting the shift to non-coercive interviewing based on the Méndez Principles.[2] Indeed, the Méndez Principles, which make a comprehensive document, are divided into six principles, namely on Foundation, on Practice, on Vulnerability, on Training, on Accountability, and on Implementation.

The principles were adopted in May 2021 by a Steering Committee of Experts with the support of the Anti-Torture Initiative, the Association for the Prevention of Torture, and the Norwegian Centre for Human Rights.[3] These are principles on effective interviewing for investigations and information gathering. The Principles on Effective Interviewing for Investigations and Information Gathering or the 'Méndez Principles' aim to modify police practices by replacing coercive interrogations with rapport-based interviews. These principles are based on science, law, and ethics, and were developed as a pathway towards a move from widespread practices of coercion-based methods to extract confessions from suspects. The results of investigations conducted through these principles are said to be improved, respectful to human rights and also enhance trust in the State.[4]

The Méndez Principles could be viewed as a more improved version of the PEACE Model, including its more advanced cognitive interviewing, in opposition to more coercive interviewing methods such as the Reid Technique.

The aims and purposes of the Méndez Principles, among many others, are basically those of preventing false confessions arising from torturous police

---

[2] www.apt.ch/news/shifting-mindsets-southern-africa-embraces-mendez-principles-effective-interviewing [access on 25 November 2024].
[3] apt_PoEI_EN_11.pdf [access on 25 April 2024].   [4] Ibid.

interviewing strategies which may lead to miscarriage of justice, among other unlawful practices. Therefore, police procedures in southern Africa are challenged to adopt this new document which is expected to improve police interviewing and also court hearings and any other investigative practices with suspects or detainees.

4.8 The Adoption of Miranda Warnings Equivalents in Southern Africa

The Miranda Warnings or Miranda Rights, which originated in the United States of America, but were later adopted by various countries, particularly those ruled by common law, such as Australia and England and Wales, where they are known as police cautions, are an important tool to mostly protect vulnerable people against self-incrimination when questioned by the police. While countries such as Mozambique, a civil law country, have not adopted these rights at all, section 35 of the 1996 South Africa Constitution[5] states a number of rights in the possession of every arrested, detained, and accused person. Though these are not called 'Miranda Rights' as such, the fact that they are enshrined in the country's Constitution could be viewed as a giant step towards the assurance of justice for all South Africans. The aforesaid rights are as follows:

(1.) Everyone who is arrested for allegedly committing an offence has the right– (a) to remain silent; (b) to be informed promptly– (i) of the right to remain silent; and (ii) of the consequence of not remaining silent; (c) not to be compelled to make any confession or admission that could be used in evidence against that person...

The same applies for Botswana, where its Criminal Procedure and Evidence Act of 1939 accords presents a law that describes the rights for suspects and the procedures police officers should follow when interviewing suspects.[6] Number 1 and 2 of the Act states as follows:

1.) A policeman may take or cause to be taken any person lawfully detained in his custody before a magistrate or any justice who is not a member of the Botswana Police Force and the magistrate or justice shall give that person the opportunity to make a statement to him in respect of any offence that person is alleged to have committed and, if that person elects to make a statement, the magistrate or justice shall record the same in writing in the language in which it is made or in some other language into which it is duly translated while being made.

---

[5] www.gov.za/sites/default/files/images/a108-96.pdf. Retrieved 10 December 2024.
[6] https://tile.loc.gov/storage-services/service/ll/llglrd/2016296556/2016296556.pdf. Retrieved 10 December 2024.

(2.) Before any person makes a statement in terms of this section, the magistrate or justice shall caution him to the effect that he is not obliged to say anything unless he wishes to do so but that should he elect to say anything it will be recorded in writing and may be used in evidence either for or against him.[7]

In the case of Malawi, the Constitution states that '[e]very person arrested for, or accused of, the alleged commission of an offence shall ... have the right –
a. promptly to be informed, in a language which he or she understands, that he or she has the right to remain silent and to be warned of the consequences of making any statement; [and] .... b. not to be compelled to make a confession or admission which could be used in evidence against him or her'.[8] Indeed, this also lies on the same framework of protecting suspects' rights.

Namibia's Criminal Procedure Act of 2004 accords suspects of a criminal act certain rights:

> 2) A member of the police conducting an investigation ... must, before questioning a person reasonably suspected of having committed an offence, give a warning explanation substantially in the following form to that person:
>
> (e) that the person to be questioned not only has the right to remain silent but also has the right to answer questions put to him or her or to give an explanation of his or her conduct or of his or her defence, if any;
>
> (f) that the person to be questioned has the right to consult a legal practitioner of his or her own choice before deciding whether or not to remain silent or to answer questions or give an explanation of his or her conduct or defence and that the legal practitioner is entitled to be present during the questioning;
>
> (g) that the warning explanation and any statement made in response thereto will be recorded in writing or mechanically and a certified copy of such recording be made available to that person ... ; and
>
> (h) that the warning explanation and any statement made in response thereto may be used in evidence in any criminal proceedings instituted against that person in respect of the offence in question, whether it be against or in favour of that person.[9]

One possible explanation for the lack of any provisions on suspects' rights such as the Miranda Warnings in countries such as Mozambique and Angola could most probably be explained by the links with its traditional civil law colonial past, on the one hand, and by the inherited common law by former British colonies, on the other hand. Nonetheless, the enforcement of Miranda Warnings by the police

---

[7] Ibid. [8] Ibid. [9] Ibid.

when interviewing suspects and detainees in the whole southern African region and beyond is more than needed for the safeguard of anyone's self-defence.

In multilingual southern African countries, one of the challenges when it comes to delivery of suspects' rights is the language of delivery of such rights, given that most people are speakers of languages, other than the official language. As these rights are mostly written in a style that even a native speaker would find it difficult to understand, an important scientific event about the delivery of suspect's rights occurred in 2016, when an international group of linguists, psychologists, lawyers, and interpreters, known as the Communication of Rights Group, drafted what are now known as Guidelines for communicating rights to non-native speakers of English in Australia, England and Wales, and the United States.[10] Despite the fact that the Guidelines were prepared for English-speaking countries, clearly the recommendations could be extended and enforced in any other country where suspects' rights are delivered. In the following lines, some of the recommendations from the Guidelines will be looked at, which are critical and their implementation in southern Africa is more than urgent.

4.8.1 Recommendation 1: Use Standardised Version in Plain English (Clear English)

The need to use plain language to avoid misunderstandings even by native speakers of the language(s) of the judicial system has long been discussed, and Gibbons (2001) demonstrated how difficult an earlier version of New South Wales police cautions would be understood even for native speakers of English in Australia. As a result, a plain language version was produced This should apply for all Southern African Countries, including those which still have not clearly adopted any suspects' rights protocol, such as Angola and Mozambique.

4.8.2 Recommendation 2: Develop Standardised Statements in Other Languages

This is clearly one of the most important recommendations as it covers multi-lingualism which is characteristic of sub-Saharan countries as a whole and southern African nations in particular. The need to have all vital documents available in the suspects' language, such as (i) information about the rights of the suspect, (ii) information about restrictions on the suspect's liberties, (iii) information about language assistance, and (iv) documents that require response from the suspect is real. According to the Guidelines, the preparation

---

[10] www.aaal.org/guidelines-for-communication-rights.

of these documents should involve bilingual lawyers, linguistic experts, and professional interpreters and translators with expertise in legal interpreting and the varieties of the languages involved. If, on the one hand, in former British colonies with some tradition of more inclusive language policies this recommendation will be more likely to implemented, Angola and Mozambique, two former Portuguese colonies with a civil law tradition as mentioned above, will still have to address other challenges related to the development of their respective indigenous languages and the approval of more inclusive language policies (see Mabasso, 2019).

4.8.3 Recommendation 3: Inform Suspects about Access to an Interpreter at the Beginning of the Interview

The need for professional interpreters to assist suspects in police interviewing in some Southern African Countries has been discussed by several scholars such as Ralarala (2014, 2019); Mabasso (2019); Heydon and Mabasso (2018); Mabasso and Heydon (2022); De Vries and Docrat (2022), just to mention a few. According to this recommendation, suspects should be told of their right to be assisted by a professional interpreter in the beginning of the interview. The target of this would be non-native speakers of any of the official languages or the language used by the judicial system. In the multilingual southern African context, this recommendation would benefit the gross majority of second language speakers, but uncertainty still remains, given the challenges with interpreting services indicated earlier.

However, in order to account for the above challenges, the recommendation is that both the interpretation and the restatement should be recorded, so that possible misinterpretation and misunderstanding or translation, or differences between the suspect's and the interpreter's dialects are avoided, thus assuring that the suspect's rights are protected and no police distortion or omission occurs (see also Gibbons, 1986, 1994).

4.8.4 Recommendation 7: Video-Record the Interview

In multilingual Southern Africa, due to the same reasons as earlier, communication of suspects' rights should be video-recorded, as countries like Tanzania have already suggested (Ngogo, 2025). This is meant to avoid that suspects end up agreeing [by saying 'yes' to the rights read before them] with something said by the police that they probably have not necessarily understood at all, thus giving room for 'vagueness' in their relevance as suspects' defence tools. However, financial constraints to implement this in most Global South nations will probably delay the effort to have this enforced.

4.9 Conclusion

As demonstrated in this section, research on police interviewing in southern Africa is still scarce, and much of the published work in the field is more related to challenges raised by police interview interpreting process (see, for example, Ralarala, 2014, 2017; De Vries & Docrat, 2022). In the two civil law countries, Angola and Mozambique, references on police interviewing can be found in the latter (Mabasso, 2019); Mabasso and Heydon (2022); and Heydon and Mabasso (2024). Given the linguistic situation, there is almost no space to draw any picture about police interviewing practices in southern Africa without connecting this to the multilingual context in which it has been developing, on the one hand, and without addressing the role of translation and interpreting, on the other hand.

This section has demonstrated that former British colonies in southern Africa have managed to combine common law tradition and customary law practices and include them in their respective constitutions, which differs from Angola and Mozambique, two civil law countries which have not formally adopted customary law as an alternative system, despite the fact that this is often used by the police when interviewing suspects (see Heydon & Mabasso, 2024). These two countries are particularly known for their sole official language policy, which hinders most suspects from defending themselves, especially when interviewed by the police, without the assistance of a qualified interpreter.

In terms of police interviewing techniques, no clear indication seems to have been provided and, most probably, police officers adopt flexible tactics to force suspects to confess, thus opening gate to coercion and corruption. One way to prevent this from happening and protect suspects' rights would be the adoption of clear police interview protocol with clearly drafted police cautions, as indicated in the 2016 recommendations by the Communication of Rights Group mentioned above, with special focus on recommendations 1, 2, 3, and 7. Translations of these recommendations should be provided in all languages spoken in each country, and, in order to ensure that these recommendations are fulfilled, individual countries should adopt monitoring strategies involving lawyers and civil society organisations. The two civil law countries, Angola and Mozambique, which still have not adopted any suspects' rights protocol, are urged to engage on this in the short time so as to comply with regional protocols such as the Implementing the Southern African Regional Police Chiefs Cooperation Organisation (SARPCCO) Code of Conduct and other vital instruments.

Given that southern African countries, through the African Commission on Human and People's Rights (ACHPR), have agreed to adopt the resolution on

The Principles on Effective Interviewing for Investigation and Information Gathering, the Méndez Principles, Southern African countries are urged to adopt these principles and, likewise, establish a monitoring mechanism of their implementation. Similar to the aforementioned recommendations, translation of these principles in the various African languages spoken in each country should be provided and the social media should play a key role in providing special programmes with a view to make the principles known to the general public.

In a multilingual and multicultural policing context such as southern Africa, successful police interviewing practices will strongly depend upon effective adoption of the available international tools and also upon how the language issue will be addressed, and here the role of qualified translators and interpreters will be essential. The section that follows brings this Element to a conclusion by charting a way forward for forensic linguistics in southern Africa.

5 Forensic Linguistics in Southern Africa: Charting Future Directions

5.1 Introduction

Article 26 (H) of the Constitution of the Republic of Zambia and Section 42(2) of the Constitution of the Republic of Malawi, for instance, stipulate that any person who is arrested or detained shall be informed the reason for the arrest in a language that they understand. Legal provisions from various countries in southern Africa guarantee that accused persons have the right to be tried in a language which they understand, or have the proceedings interpreted to them in a language which they understand. These provisions are crucial in foregrounding the institutionalisation of the importance of language in law and legal proceedings in southern Africa. Therefore, despite the fact that forensic linguistics is in its infancy and in formative stages, as a distinct field of inquiry, in most of southern African countries, this section charts the future direction of forensic linguistics in the region by using data from Malawi, Zimbabwe, Namibia, Kenya, Tanzania, Zambia, and South Africa. This supports the data already put forward in Section 1 of this Element. In this section, we present plausible strategies that once taken on board can assure the growth of forensic linguistics in the region. However, before we do so, the first two subsections outline the institutionalisation and the current status of forensic linguistics in the selected countries, the existing gaps, the leading scholars, and some important publications that have pushed forensic linguistics forward.

Information from Malawi, Zimbabwe, and South Africa was obtained from academic publications, while the discussion from Kenya, Namibia, Tanzania, and

Zambia is based on formally solicited reports from some leading scholars in the field. These reports were obtained from Dr Humphrey Kapau (Zambia), Prof Emmanuel Satia (Kenya) Patricia Muriguri (Tanzania); and Prof Haileleul Zeleke Woldermariam (Namibia). However, both information obtained from academic published and reports from individual scholars point out to the fact that forensic linguistics remains largely untapped to the extent that a search through various repositories with the tagline 'forensic linguistics' would yield very little, if anything, as the existing works have not yet been explicitly labelled as forensic linguistics.

5.2 Institutionalisation of Forensic Linguistics and the Current Trend in the Region

5.2.1 Kenya

In Kenya, serious engagement in forensic linguistics started about fifteen years when Ogone John Obiero (now Professor) won the Malcolm Coulthard 2009 Award to attend the International Association of Forensic Linguistics (IAFL) Conference. Later, works by Kiguru (2010) and Odhiambo, Kavulani, and Matu (2013a) appeared as articles in different non-forensic linguistics journals. But it is Satia (2012) who appears in the Proceedings of the Biennial IAFL Conference for the IAFL Conference in Birmingham. In 2017, like Ogone, Esther Kimani won the Prof Roger Shuy Award to attend the IAFL Conference in Porto, Portugal, to present a paper on the 'Dis-honourable Suspect'. As a discipline, forensic linguistics is taught at two universities – Moi University and the University of Nairobi – with Moi University offering courses at both undergraduate and postgraduate levels.

5.2.2 Malawi

Since the introduction of forensic linguistics in Malawi in 2015, the country has registered significant growth of the discipline both in terms of research and as a field of study. The forensic linguistics module, which is being offered at the undergraduate level at Mzuzu University, continues to inspire students to pursue the field further. The master's programme in applied linguistics (law enforcement discourse), which is being offered at the same university and had its first intake in 2022, has been an attractive programme to candidates from diverse backgrounds. The programme, which had its first intake enrolment of nineteen, the second intake of eighteen, and the third intake of thirty candidates, has attracted and brought together students with backgrounds such as linguistics, security studies, law, police, law enforcement, human rights, and communication studies. This wider scope of students is a promising development, and it shows the exponential growth of the field and its sustainability.

Furthermore, research outputs that are largely initiated and authored by Kondowe, which have been shared widely, have also helped in making the nation aware about the existence of forensic linguistics and its relevance in solving legal problems. Of late, some of the postgraduate students have also started publishing in the field (see Lungu, 2025; Zoloni & Ndalama-Mtawali, 2025). We have also started witnessing research outputs from legal professionals who have started publishing in legal linguistics. Some of their studies address challenges that vulnerable witnesses such as children experience in court. These studies provide lived experiences that legal professionals observe as they discharge their duties (See Chirwa, 2025; NyaKaunda, 2025; Kondowe & nyaKaunda, 2025; Soko & Kondowe, 2025). Recently, the Attorney General of Malawi graced the symposium where the postgraduate students showcased their research works and how such studies contribute to the Malawi 2063 Agenda. Therefore, even though the discipline was started at Mzuzu University, there is clear visibility of the increased number of students and legal professionals interested in the field of forensic linguistics.

5.2.3 Tanzania

Contrary to the developments registered in Kenya and Malawi, in Tanzania, so far there is no university that offers forensic linguistics as part of their linguistic programmes or as a study on its own. Forensic analysis of language in Tanzania is classed under the forensic sciences. The centralised criminal record unit was initiated in 1953 under the British colonial rule and initially it centred on archiving of fingerprints, but in 1960 the Photographic, Questioned Document, Crime Scene Management and Ballistics sections were introduced. The Forensic Bureau of Tanzania was established under the police force to handle matters requiring forensic examination. Currently, the Questioned Document Laboratory (QDL) of the Forensic Bureau of Tanzania Police Force deals with crimes including handwriting, signatures, forgery, counterfeits, rubber stamp marks, paper marks, ink analysis, and restorations of erased documents in combating crimes and providing evidence before the court of law.

In Tanzania, members of the Police force are trained to conduct such forensic investigation, and they are gazetted; therefore, the Courts receive evidence from gazetted forensic investigators only. The curriculum used in training the experts is specific to the police college and only recently universities (University of Dar es salaam) have started offering criminology programmes. It cannot be established whether the police officers dealing with forensic analysis of language are linguists. According to an online article written in *The Citizen*, Tanzania's forensic services are hampered by the presence of few experts and lack of certification and accreditation of laboratories. Only the Government Chemist Laboratory Authority (GCLA) is ISO-compliant. The report on the review of evidence law in Tanzania states that documentary evidence presents special problems not presented by other forms of real evidence. They propose that in order to authenticate such documents material alterations should be accounted for and any acknowledgement proved, and in addition to that, self-authentication can also be considered for some documents. The procedures for authentication and identification of material alterations are not set out in the Evidence Law, and the assumption is that the expert will use his or her experience to attain this.

5.2.4 Namibia

In Namibia, forensic linguistics started through the establishment of Forensic Stylistics as part of Stylistics between 2017 and 2023. In January 2017, the Department of Communication and Languages at the Namibia University of Science and Technology launched the Master of English and Applied Linguistics (MEAL) programme at NQF level 9. As part of this curriculum, the Department included 'Forensic Stylistics' as an integral part of Stylistics. Forensic Stylistics, as a chapter of its own, was studied as a branch of Applied Linguistics that applied analytical techniques to legal and criminal issues. It involved a forensic stylistic analysis of written or spoken materials to determine and measure content, meaning, speaker identification, or determination of authorship in the Namibian legal contexts. Consequently, the following MEAL candidates/graduates and their supervisors ventured to add forensic stylistics research projects in the Land of the Braves for the first time. Six students graduated under this programme.

Much of the support regarding the growth of forensic linguistics in Namibia has been supported by postgraduate students from January 2024, who are equipped with both theoretical and practical skills necessary to analyse and critique language use in diverse legal contexts and compare and evaluate practical applications of linguistic methods to legal problems; the Department introduced forensic linguistics as an independent course into the revised Master of English and Applied Linguistics (MOEL) programme. This new course is hands-on and research-based, and allows candidates to critically assess cases involving prominent Namibian figures, famous Namibian/South African brand names, and highly contested authorship attribution disputes in Namibia and beyond. This course, therefore, outlines the linguistic aspects of legal contexts and the relevance of linguistic theories to forensic problems, describes and critiques the main theoretical and research trajectories within forensic linguistics research, and provides practical skills in analysing and interpreting texts in forensic settings. By examining actual litigated cases involving interpretation (notably defamation), trademark (infringement and genericide), and authorship, this course helps prepare candidates to do real-life research in forensic linguistics.

5.2.5 Zimbabwe

There has been slow development of forensic linguistics in Zimbabwe largely because the discipline has not been established as a field of study in the country. Out of twelve universities that Svongoro and Ralarala (2023) surveyed, only five had some forensic linguistics–related course offerings, though not fully specialised in forensic linguistics. As noted by Svongoro and Ralarala (2023), no university in Zimbabwe has developed a degree programme exclusively focusing on forensic linguistics. The five universities indirectly comprised some courses that have a bearing on forensic linguistics education. In addition, the absence of Zimbabwean researchers at major regional and international conferences in forensic linguistics has resulted in the dearth of publications on the discipline. It was also noted that there is resistance by some language departments in establishing forensic linguistics–related programmes, largely due to a shortage of trained forensic and legal linguists in the country. Zimbabwean universities therefore feel themselves to be incapacitated to develop and teach forensic linguistics. So far, only a very few researchers have researched and published in the field. Some of these scholars include Eventhough Ndlovu, Patson Kufakunesu, Paul Svongoro, and Josemuta Mutangadura.

5.3 Forensic Linguistics Research Studies in Southern Africa

Just like in the growth of the discipline itself, research studies in forensic linguistics in the Southern African region have been so lean. The major growth of research has been the movement which is led by University of the Western Cape in South Africa which is led by Professor Monwabisi Ralarala and Professor Russell Kaschula. The movement has given rise to the book series in *Studies in Forensic and Legal Linguistics in Africa and Beyond* which has so far led to the publication of six book volumes. However, not much research has been registered in individual countries.

5.3.1 Tanzania

There are a handful of publications in Tanzania largely led by Patricia Muraguri who is an assistant lecturer at Mbeya University of Science and Technology and is currently pursuing her PhD at Moi University in Kenya. Some of the notable publications in Tanzania include 'Ranking of Descriptors for Complainants Based on Perceived Victimhood' (Muraguri & Satia, 2023) AND 'An Examination of the Terms Used to Describe Sexual Assault in Written Judicial Opinions' (Muraguri, Nganga, & Satia, 2024). There is also Dr Frolence Rutechura of the University of Dar es salaam who has also indicated forensic linguistics as his specialty on his profile. There are also A few appearances in international conference presentations from Tanzania such as the Language Association of Eastern Africa (LAEA) conference in Uganda (August 2023); International Sociological Association (ISA); and the DUNACOSTI conference at Daystar University. Nairobi. 2021.

5.3.2 Malawi

In the past, forensic linguistics did not enjoy much scholarly attention in Malawi perhaps because the field was not yet known. One of the earlier works that have been noticed is the one by Kishindo (2001) which interrogated 'the use of indigenous languages in [Malawian] courts'. But later, since 2022, there have been some remarkable works published in the field. Some of them include 'An Intentional Insincerity in Witnesses' Discursive Strategies' (Kondowe, Liao, & Ngwira, 2022); 'Insincerity in Lawyer's Questioning Strategies' (Kondowe, 2023); 'The Principle of Believability in Forensic Settings' (Kondowe, 2022); 'Interruptions as Linguistic Whistles' (Kondowe & Mtanga, 2023); 'Entrenching Effective Multilingualism in Malawian Courtrooms through Interpreting Services' (Lwara, Kondowe, & Mtawali, 2024); 'Impersonalisation as a Stance-taking Strategy in the Writing of Judgements' (Kondowe & Lwara, 2025); and 'Linguist as an Expert Witness' (Kondowe & Ngwira, 2025). Kishindo has currently co-edited three book volumes which are an important contribution to the field in Southern Africa, namely, *Multilingualism in Southern Africa* (Routledge; 2024); *The Language of Violence and Crime in the Global South* (Sun Press); and *Discrimination and Access to Justice in Africa* (Routledge).

As mentioned earlier, we have also witnessed publications from legal professionals. Some of them are 'Linguistic Barriers to Access to Justice by Child Victims and Witnesses of Sexual Assault' (Chirwa, 2025); 'The Application of Language and Procedural Entitlements of Children in Detention' (nyaKaunda Kamanga, 2025); and 'Narrative Navigation in Legal Persuasion' (Kondowe & nyaKaunda, 2025). Some of the postgraduate students have also published scholarly works. For instance, 'Legal Status of Malawi Sign Language and Its

Implications on Access to Justice for the Deaf' (Zoloni & Ndalama-Mtawali, 2025) and 'Language, Power and Voice Loss in the Discourse of Lawyers and Witnesses' (Lungu, 2025). All these works bring optimism that the field of forensic linguistics is gaining ground and becoming established in Malawi.

5.3.3 Zambia

In Zambia, there is an awareness newspaper weekly column called 'Language and You: Facts and Myths' in *The Mast* newspaper where public awareness on linguistics in general is made through newspaper articles (Kapau, 2021a). *The Mast* is the only newspaper column in Zambia that has talked on a number of topics related to forensic linguistics to raise public awareness on the field and on language and linguistics in general. The column has attracted a wide range of readers in and outside Zambia. In the article 'Forensic Linguistics and the Handwriting of Crime Suspects' (Kapau, 2021a), the newspaper talks about the linguistic properties of handwriting and how handwriting features make forensic linguistics an indispensable field in providing insights to a crime scene. Kapau (2021b) also explores the role of forensic semiotics and forensic psycholinguistics in consolidating forensic linguistics in identifying crime in nonverbal communication. The article carefully navigates the borderline nature of forensic semiotics and forensic psychology to explore the independence of forensic semiotics from psychology. In the article, body language kinesics (body movement communication); haptics (communication by touch); vocalics (communication by voice); proxemics (communication by space and distance); chronemics (communication by time); personal appearance; and physical environment are linked to verbal language aspects of linguistics nature and paralinguistic features, in the context of crime identification.

5.4 Charting Future Directions

The earlier discussion has brought to the fore a number of challenges that southern African countries are facing in relation to the introduction and the growth of forensic linguistics in the region. Some of the key challenges highlighted include low research output, lack of qualified staff in forensic linguistics, limited number of universities teaching forensic linguistics, lack of accreditation and certification of linguists' experts, and attitudes of some departments towards the discipline. Despite these shortcomings, the field is still developing in the region, with some optimistic advancements expected as the field becomes better understood and institutionalised. Reports obtained from leading scholars in various countries provide remarkable evidence that forensic linguistics has the potential to thrive despite its current weak status. Zambia and

South Africa, for instance, have already started demonstrating the working relationship between law enforcement agencies and forensic linguists, where forensic linguistics are being put into practice to solve practical problems in law. These are just some of the few countries that have begun applying linguistic insights in legal contexts. This emerging intersection of language and law is an assurance on the future of the discipline. Our key informant in Zambia reported that, during the time this Element was written, there were six active cases involving the State and some high-profile Zambian politicians in which the State sought the help of language experts to help provide services involving linguistic knowledge. These are experts in linguistics, particularly from the Department of Arts, Language, and Literary Studies at the University of Zambia, who are leading the way by providing linguistic insights into legal matters and collaborating with various stakeholders.

In Kenya, although there is no documented involvement of forensic linguists in courtroom practice or any other forensic linguistics–related work as experts, the future of the discipline seems assured. More research on forensic linguistics is coming out, and there are working groups on WhatsApp platforms under the aegis of the African Association for Forensic and Legal Linguistics (AAFLL). Furthermore, new developments that have seen the Directorate of Criminal Investigations (DCI) open up a state-of-the–art forensic laboratory at its headquarters gives hope that in the not-so-distant future, the expertise of forensic linguists will be sought if the practicing forensic linguistics experts work to demonstrate the value of their work to relevant security agencies such as the National Police Service, the DCI, the Ethics & Anti-Corruption Commission (EACC), the National Intelligence Service (NIS) as well as the National Cohesion and Integration Commission (NCIC).

Similarly, some positive developments have also been witnessed in Zimbabwe regarding the teaching, research, and forensic linguistics education. First, Svongoro and Ralarala's (2023) report on postgraduate students who have demonstrated a keen interest in research on language use in police stations and courtrooms when researching for their dissertations and projects respectively. Secondly, some Zimbabweans have enrolled and completed postgraduate degrees with South African universities, majoring in language practice, translation, and interpreting, with some majoring in court interpretation. There is also an increase in research and publications in such areas as court interpreting, interpreting in the parliament, and language rights (see Svongoro & Wallmach, 2019; Ndlovu, 2020; Kufakunesu & Svongoro, 2023).

The introduction of the Master of Arts in Applied Linguistics (Law Enforcement Discourse) at Mzuzu University in Malawi is also a big development which gives a promising future for forensic linguistics in the region.

Nineteen students were recruited in the first cohort. The second group comprised eighteen students, while the third intake comprises thirty students. Such growing numbers of students in each intake demonstrate that forensic linguistics has become an attractive discipline of study. What is more fascinating about the situation in Malawi is that the programme is bringing together police, army, lawyers, judicial offers, and linguists which is the first of its kinds since these fields have existed in isolation for many decades. This has been possible because of the name of the programme which was crafted to attract a wider audience with both law and linguistics backgrounds. Further, it has been reported that legal professionals are now able to appreciate the gaps in their profession which need linguistic interventions. In a study done by Kondowe and Ngwira (2024) which investigated knowledge and altitude of legal professionals towards the involvement of linguists' experts in court, legal professionals expressed positive knowledge about the services of language experts. However, they were not sure where this expertise can be found since they have never heard about their availability in Malawi. This shows that forensic linguists in the region do not make their expertise available on the ground. Southern African universities, therefore, need to start producing applied linguists who can work as expert witnesses and be of service during police investigations, and provide superior knowledge in trial processes that centre on the question of language. Even though Zambia and South Africa have started showing some positive movement in this direction, most African countries are still behind.

One of the major achievements in forensic linguistics research in southern Africa is that there has been a balance of studies covering almost all aspects of forensic linguistics from both students and academics. For instance, there are studies on courtroom discourse, court interpreting, police interviews, language policies, forensic linguistic evidence, linguists as expert witness. This is contrary to the situation in the Philippines, where Ranosa-Madrunio and Martin (2023) lament the limited focus on forensic linguistic evidence studies. Studies in linguistic evidence are those that are concerned with trademark linguistics, plagiarism detection, text messaging forensics, authorship attribution, suicide notes, fraud, phishing, and others. These studies are the ones that directly require the expertise of forensic linguists when such cases are at both investigative and trial stages. Studies in southern Africa are well spread in all these areas. However, the major challenge is that police and courts do hardly engage the expertise of linguists, not because they are not available, but because their expertise is hardly appreciated. Research studies in linguistic evidence are the pillar if forensic linguistics is to be appreciated in the region. Just like forensic pathology, entomology, dactyloscopy, and computational forensics, forensic linguistic evidence has heuristic potential in enhancing the delivery of justice. For this to be successful, linguists' experts need certification and accreditation by established bodies so that they can execute their expertise with greatest recognition.

One of the first key issues that the region is battling with at the moment is discrimination and vulnerability of its citizens once they come in contact with the law which is a westernised system. In their edited book volume, *Discrimination and Access to Justice in Africa: Language, Vulnerability and Social Inclusion in Southern and Eastern Africa*, Kondowe and Svongoro (2025) puts together various works from the Southern and Eastern Africa region that document different forms of vulnerability experienced by children, women, intoxicated witnesses, the poor and the illiterate, unrepresented litigants, the hearing impaired, witnesses with mental disorders, foreigners, and migrants which block their access to justice. By drawing from case studies from Malawi, Zimbabwe, Kenya, Tanzania, South Africa, and Zambia, it is noted that southern African countries adopted formal or state judicial systems based on Western customs which are products of colonialism. These westernised method of resolving disputes are strange to the majority of Africans resulting in various forms of discrimination when citizens participate in the justice system. What comes out clear is that justice systems in South African countries face similar challenges such as lack of qualified court interpreters, use of foreign languages, lack of recognition of sign language, discriminatory legal provisions, and poverty. Therefore, forensic linguists on the African continent need to come up with practical solutions of alleviating language-induced vulnerability so that everyone receives fair treatment in line with international human rights law regardless of their condition.

Multilingualism remains one of the major challenges in most (if not all) southern African countries. Justice systems in most countries are struggling with colonial inherited practices where both the language of record and the language of practice remain English. A recent study done in Malawi has exposed poor court interpreting where the interpreters remain untrained bilinguals and communication gets distorted, thus affecting true justice from emerging (Lwara, Kondowe, & Ndalama, 2024). The same challenges are also witnessed in police formations where police officers who are not professional translators translate into English witness statements originally spoken in local languages. Therefore, southern African countries should consider developing and incorporating AI software that can support interpretation both at police stations and in courts. These can be translation apps, online legal dictionaries, and hearing aid machines that can facilitate the communication process with various groups, including those with hearing impairments, foreign language speakers, and witnesses with communication discoursers. An alternative approach would be to advocate for a decolonised justice system that should use local language, unless in exceptional cases where the litigants and court officials do not share a common language. This can further be supported by first introducing law as a compulsory subject in early education levels so that the law is not seen to be strange to the people who should obey it.

5.5 Conclusion

Forensic linguistics can have a strong future and be impactful if the discipline is also directly taught to law students. The University of the Western Cape (UWC) in South Africa has successfully started offering forensic linguistics in the Faculty of Law. In Malawi, law graduates are being enrolled in the MA programme in applied linguistics (law enforcement discourse). These are success stories to prove that legal education is insufficient when it is deprived of linguistics. Further, unlike Malawi, South Africa, and Kenya, who have introduced postgraduate programmes in forensic linguistics, most African countries are still lagging behind. If forensic linguistics is to be impactful in the region, there is a need for every country to have a postgraduate programme. The lack of expertise should not be used as an excuse to deprive the nation. Mzuzu University in Malawi started the postgraduate programme with one member of staff specialised in the field, but through partnerships with UWC, the programme took off and is growing fast. Apart from the postgraduate programme, universities should also open up their spaces for short-term training in different aspects of forensic linguistics which should target law enforcement agencies. These strategies are important as we chart the future direction of forensic linguistics in southern Africa to improve efficiency in the delivery of justice in the region.

References

Ansah, M. A. & Darko, P. O. 2019. Justice in the mother tongue. In Ralarala, M. K., Kaschula, R. H., & Heydon, G. (eds.). *New Frontiers in Forensic Linguistics*: *Themes and Perspectives in Language and Law in Africa and beyond*. Stellenbosch: African Sun Media. 113:113–146.

Atindogbé, G. G. & Dissake, E. M. K. 2019. Forensic linguistics as a tool for the development of Cameroon national languages: The case of Tunen. *African Study Monographs*, 40(1): 23–44.

Ayogu, I. I. & Olutayo, V. A. 2016. Authorship attribution using rough sets-based feature selection technique. *International Journal of Computer Applications*, 152(6):38–46. https://doi.org/10.5120/ijca2016911889.

Babarinde, O. & Oku, E. 2020. Language variation and stylistics in criminal profiling and authorship attribution. *IKENGA International Journal of Institute of African Studies*, 18(1): 174–182.

Babili, G. L. 2024. Police interviews in a non-native context: Misconstructions and possible solutions. *Southern African Linguistics and Applied Language Studies*, 42(1): S53–S66, DOI: 10.2989/16073614.2023.2288882.

Bamgbose, A. 1991. *Language and the Nation*: *The Language Question in Sub-Saharan Africa*. Edinburgh: Edinburg University Press.

Barak, M. 2021. Can you hear me now? Attorney perceptions of interpretation, technology, and power in immigration court. *Journal on Migration and Human Security*, 9(4): 233150242110347. https://doi.org/10.1177/23315024211034740.

Bathia, V. 1994. Cognitive structuring in legislative provisions. In Gibbons, J. (ed.). *Language and the Law*. London: Longman. 136–155.

Batibo, H. M. & Smieja, B. (eds.). 2000. *Botswana*: *The Future of Minority Languages*. Berlin: Peter Lang.

Berk-Seligson, S. 2009. Coerced confessions: The discourse of bilingual police interrogations. *International Journal of Speech Language and the Law*, 17(1):171–176.

Brohy, C., du Plesssis, T., Turi, J. G., & Woehrling, J. (eds.). 2013. *Law, Language and the Multilingual State. Proceedings of the 12th International Conference of the International Academy of Linguistic Law*. Stellenbosch: African Sun Media. 269–290.

Cassim, F. 2003. The right to address the court in the language of one's choice. *Codicillus*, 44(2):24–31.

Chawinga, W. D., Kapondera, S. K., Chipeta, G. T., Majawa, F., & Nyasulu, C. 2019. Towards e-judicial services in Malawi: Implications for justice delivery. *The Electronic Journal of Information Systems in Developing Countries*, 86:1–15, e12121. https://doi.org/10.1002/isd2.12121.

Chimbutane, F. 2015. Bilingual education: Enabling classroom interaction and bridging the gap between schools and rural communities in Mozambique. *International Journal of Educational Development in Africa*, 2(1):101–120.

Chimbutane, F. 2016. Multilingual resources in Classroom interaction: Portuguese and African/Creole languages in monolingual and bilingual education programs. *Springer International Publishing*. www.researchgate.net/publication/313014009_Multilingual_Resources_in_Classroon_Interaction. Access on 27 May 2020.

Chirwa, O. S. 2025. Linguistic barriers to access to justice by child victims and witnesses of sexual assault in Malawi's justice system. In Kondowe, W. & Svongoro. P. (eds.). *Discrimination and Access to Justice in Africa: Language, Vulnerability and Social Inclusion in Southern and Eastern Africa*. New York: Routledge. 25–36.

Claudio, F. 2018. Interpreting and technology: The upcoming technological turn. In Fantinuoli, C. (ed.). *Interpreting and Technology*. Berlin: Language Science Press. 1–12. https://doi.org/10.5281/zenodo.1493289.

De Vries, A. & Docrat, Z. 2019. Multilingualism in the South African legal system. In Ralarala, M. K., Kaschula, R. H., & Heydon, G. (eds.). *New Frontiers in Forensic Linguists: Themes and Perspectives in Language and Law in Africa and beyond*. Stellenbosch: SUN PRESS. 89–112.

De Vries, A. & Docrat, Z. 2022. Judges and court interpreters' experiences of multilingualism in South African courts. In Ralarala, M. K., Kaschula, R. H., & Heydon, G. (eds.). *Language and the Law Global Perspectives in Forensic Linguistics from Africa and beyond*. Stellenbosch: African Sun Media. 101–123.

Dissake, E. M. K. 2021. *Language and Legal Proceedings: Analysing Courtroom Discourse in Cameroon*. Switzerland: Palgrave.

Dissake, E. M. K. 2022. Assessing litigant's' language proficiency: The case of the Bafoussam Court of first instance. *Language Policy*, 21(2): 217–234.

Dissel, A., & Frank, C. (eds.). 2012. Policing and Human Rights: Assessing southern African countries' compliance with the SARPCCO Code of Conduct for Police Officials. African Civil Oversighting Forum. https://apcof.org/wp-content/uploads/2016/05/Policing-and-Human-Rights-assessing-Southern-African-Countries-compliance-with-the-SARPCCO-Code-of-Conduct-1.pdf [Accessed 10 December 2024].

Docrat, Z. 2017. The role of African languages in the South of African legal system: Towards a transformative agenda. Unpublished Master's Thesis. Grahamstown: Rhodes University.

Docrat, Z. 2019. A critique of the language of record in South African courts in relation to selected university language policies. PhD Thesis. Grahamstown: Rhodes University.

Docrat, Z. 2022. A review of linguistic qualifications and training for legal professionals and judicial officers: A call for linguistic equality in South Africa's legal profession. *International Journal for the Semiotics of Law*, 35: 1711–1731. https://doi.org/10.1007/s11196-022-09902-9.

Docrat, Z., & Kaschula, R. H. 2019. Onolingual language of record: A critique of South Africa's new policy directive. In Kaschula, R.H., Ralarala, M., & Heydon, G. (eds.). *New Frontiers in Forensic Linguistics: Themes and Perspectives in Language and the Law in Africa and Beyond*. Stellenbosch: SUN Press. 71–88.

Docrat, Z. & de Vries, A. 2022. Judges and court interpreters' experiences of multilingualism in South African courts. In Ralarala, M., Kaschula, R. H., & Heydon, G. (eds.). *Language and the Law: Global Perspectives in Forensic Linguistics from Africa and beyond*. Stellenbosch: African Sun Media. 101–121. https://doi.org/10.52779/9781991201836/05.

Docrat, Z., & Kaschula, R. H. 2024. Cultural and linguistic prejudices experienced by African language speaking witnesses and legal practitioners at the hands of judicial officers in South African courtroom discourse: The Senzo Meyiwa murder trial. *International Journal of the Semiotics of Law*, 37:1309–1322. https://doi.org/10.1007/s11196-023-10071-6.

Docrat, Z., Kaschula, R. H., & Ralarala, M. K. 2021. *A Handbook on Legal Languages and the Quest for Linguistic Equality in South Africa and beyond*. Stellenbosch: African Sun Media.

Donovan, P., & Perez, P. 2024. Interviewing techniques in 11 Sub-saharan Arican nations. In Walsh, D., Bull, R., & Areh, I. (eds.). *Routledge Handbook of Investigative Interviewing and Interrogation*. London and New York: Routledge. 294–319.

Fares, F. 2023. Exploring the language of investigation: A forensic linguistics approach. https://dspace.univ-temouchent.edu.dz/handle/123456789/3380.

Gibbons, J. 1986. Courtroom application of second language acquisition research. *Australian Review of Applied Linguistics*, (3):131–133. https://doi.org/10.1075/aealss.3.09gib.

Gibbons, J. 1994. *Language and the Law*. London: Longman. https://doi.org/10.1177%2F096394709500400207.

Gibbons, J. 2001. Revising the language of New South Wales police procedures: Applied Linguistics in action. *Applied Linguistics*, 22(4):439–470.

Gibbons, J. 2003. *Forensic Linguistics: An Introduction to Language in the Justice System*. Oxford: Blackwell.

Gloria, C. P. 2018. Tools for interpreters: The challenges that lie ahead. *Current Trends in Translation Teaching and Learning*, 5:157–182.

Government of the Republic of Mozambique. 2004. Constitution of the Republic of Mozambique (revised 2007). Government of the Republic of Mozambique.

Government of the Republic of Zimbabwe. 2013. Constitution of Zimbabwe Amendment (No. 20) Act, 2013. Harare: Government Printers.

Hale, S. B. 2021. Themes and methodological issues in Court Interpreting research. *Linguistica antverpiensia new series – Themes in Translation Studies*. https://doi.org/10.52034/lanstts.v5i.161.

Hanekom, J. 2021. Investigative interviewing from an intercultural communication perspective: A theoretical frame-work to guide law enforcers in South Africa. https://hdl.handle.net/10520/ejc-ajcj_v6_n1_a5. [Accessed 10 DEcember 2024].

Heugh, K. 2003. *Language policy and democracy in South Africa*. Centre for Research on Bilingualism. Stockholm University: Stockholm University Press.

Heydon G. & Mabasso, E. 2018. The impact of multilingualism on reporting domestic violence in Mozambique. *Language Matters*, 49(1):84–106. https://doi.org/10.1080/10228195.2018.1444081.

Heydon, G. & Mabasso, E. 2024. Mozambican police and judicial investigative interviewing. In Walsh, D. & Areh, I. (eds.). *Routledge International Handbook of Investigative Interviewing and Interrogation*. London and New York: Routledge. 363–385.

Hubbard, E. H. 1994. Errors in court: A forensic application of error analysis. *SA Journal of Linguistics*, (20): 3–16.

Hubbard, E. H. 1995. Linguistic fingerprinting: A case study in forensic linguistics. *SA Journal of Linguistics*, (26), 55–72.

International Association of Forensic Linguists. 2014. British Council Tunisia.

Issa, A. C. M., Garcia, I., Jeque, N., & Timbane, T. 2010. *Código de Processo Civil* (com Alterações introduzidas). Maputo: Unidade Técnica de Reforma Legal.

Joshua, U. 2023. Forensic linguistics and language issues in multilingual-oriented legal discourse. *International Journal of Multilingualism and Languages for Specific Purposes*, 5(1):11–32.

Kamweru, N. 2016. Controlling courtroom discourse through linguistic manipulation: A case study of criminal trials at the Kibera law courts. Unpublished MA thesis. Nairobi: Catholic University of Eastern Africa.

Kapau, H. M. 2021a. Forensic linguistics vs handwriting of crime suspects. *The Mast Newspaper*. (In hardcopy).

Kapau, H. M. 2021b. Signs of crime: Body language of liars. *The Mast Newspaper*. (29 June, In hardcopy).

Kapau, H. M. 2021c. Detecting political liars through forensic linguistics. *The Mast Newspaper*. (28 July. In hardcopy).

Kaschula, R. H. 2021. *Languages, Identities and Intercultural Communication in South Africa and beyond*. London: Routledge.

Kaschula, R. H. & Ralarala, M. K. 2004. Language rights, intercultural communication and the law in South Africa. *South African Journal of African Languages*, 4(24):252–261. https://doi.org/10.1080/02572117.2004.10587242.

Kaschula, R. H. & Wolff, E. H. 2016. *Multilingual Education for Africa: Concepts and Practices*. Pretoria: UNISA Press; London and New York: Routledge.

Kaschula, R.H., Ralarala, M.K. & Heydon, G. (Eds.) (2023). *Language, Crime and the Courts in South Africa and Beyond*. Stellenbosch: African Sun Media.

Kasonde, A. 2017. The changing role of the court interpreter-translator in Africa: The case of Zambia. *Comparative Legilinguistics*, 27(1):21–32.

Kembo Sure, K. & Satia, E. 2017. Language crimes: The grammar and vocabulary of hate speech in Kenya. *Mwanga wa Lugha*, 1(1):21–38.

Kengni, B. & and Nkosi, V. 2023. Analysis of the current legal framework protecting the health of communities near gold mine tailings in South Africa. *Southern African Public Law*. 37(22):1–19. https://doi.org/10.25159/2522-6800/12919.

Khati, T. 2001. Multilingualism and the judiciary in Lesotho: The challenges of the 21st century. In Deprez, K., Du Plessis, T., & Teck, L. (eds.). *Multilingualism, the Judiciary and Security Services: Belgium, Europe, South Africa, Southern Africa*. Pretoria: Van Schaik. 167–177.

Kiguru, G. 2010. At the mercy of others' voices: An illustration of frequent interpreter language errors in Kenyan courtrooms. *The University of Nairobi Journal of Languages and Linguistics*, 1:1–8.

Kimani, E. W., Satia, E., & Kembo-Sure, E. 2022. Self-representation in the opening statements of the confirmation-of-charges hearing of the ICC-Kenya case one. In Ralarala, M. K., Kaschula, R. H., & Heydon, G. (eds.). *Language and the Law: Global Perspectives in Forensic Linguistics from Africa and beyond*. Stellenbosch: African Sun Media. 279–296.

Kishindo, P. 2001. Language and the law in Malawi: A case for the use of indigenous languages in the legal system. *Language Matters: Studies in the Languages of Africa*, 32(1):1–27. https://doi.org/10.1080/10228190108566170.

Kondowe, W. 2022. Towards the principle of believability: A new socio-pragmatic model in forensic settings. In Ralarala, M. K., Kaschula, R. H., & Heydon, G. (eds.). *Language and the Law*: *Global Perspectives in Forensic Linguistics from Africa and beyond*. Stellenbosch: African Sun Media. 261–278. https://doi.org/10.52779/9781991201836/13.

Kondowe, W. 2023. Insincerity in lawyers' questioning strategies in Malawian criminal courtroom discourse. *Text & Talk* (aop). https://doi.org/10.1515/text-2022-0083.

Kondowe, W. & Mtanga, G. 2023. Interruptions as linguistic whistles: An examination of the language of judges in Malawian courtroom discourse. In Kaschula, R. H., Ralarala, M. K., & Heydon, G. (eds.). *Language, Crime and the Courts in South Africa and beyond*. Stellenbosch: African Sun Media. 33–50.

Kondowe, W. & Ngwira, F. F. 2024. Linguist as an expert witness: Knowledge, attitude and perceived importance of legal professionals in Malawi. In Ralarala, M. K. Kaschula, R. H., & Docrat. Z. (eds.). *Documenting Forensic Linguistics in the African Context*: *Perspectives in language and legal practice*. Stellenbosch: African Sun Media. 1–22.

Kondowe, W., & Lwara, E. 2025. Interrogating the language of law in Malawi: A study of impersonalisation as a stance-taking strategy in the writing of judgements for criminal trials. In Ralarala, M.K. Kaschula, R.H., & Docrat. Z. (eds.). *Documenting Forensic Linguistics in the African Context: Perspectives in language and legal practice*. Stellenbosch: Sun Press. 211–226.

Kondowe, W., & Ngwira, F. F. 2025. Linguist as an expert witness: Knowledge, Attitude and Perceived importance of Legal professionals in Malawi. In Ralarala, M.K. Kaschula, R.H., & Docrat. Z. (eds.). *Documenting Forensic Linguistics in the African Context*: *Perspectives in language and legal practice*. Stellenbosch: Sun Press.189–210.

Kondowe, W. & nyaKaunda Kamanga, D. 2025. Narrative navigation in legal persuasion: A rhetorical analysis of lawyers' affidavits and skeleton arguments for appellate relief in criminal cases in Malawi. *Text & Talk* (aop) (in press). https://doi.org/10.1515/text-2023-0230.

Kondowe, W. & Svongoro. P. (eds.). (2025). *Discrimination and Access to Justice in Africa: Language, Vulnerability and Social Inclusion in Southern and Eastern Africa*. New York: Routledge.

Kondowe, W., Kamanga, C. M. M., & Madula, P. (eds.). 2024. *Multilingualism in Southern Africa*: *Issues and Perspectives*. New York: Routledge. https://doi.org/10.4324/9781003461708.

Kondowe, W., Liao, M., & Ngwira, F. F. 2022. A study of intentional insincerity in Malawian criminal justice: Witnesses' discursive strategies. In M. K. Ralarara,

R. H. Kaschula, & G. Heydon (eds.). *Language and the Law: Global Perspectives in Forensic Linguistics from Africa and beyond*. Stellenbosch: African Sun Press. 241–260.

Kotzé, E. F. 2007. Die vangnet van die woord: Forensies-linguistiese getuienis in 'n lastersaak. *Southern African Linguistics and Applied Language Studies*, 25(3): 385–399.

Kotzé, E. F. 2010. Author identification from opposing perspectives in forensic linguistics. *Southern Africa Linguistics and Applied Language Studies*, 28(2): 185–197.

Kretzer, M. & Kaschula, R. H. 2022. *Handbook of Language Policy and Education in Countries of the Southern African Development Community (SADC)*. Leiden: BRILL.

Kufakunesu, P. & Svongoro, P. 2023. Some methodological issues in language research: Dealing with transcribed interpreted courtroom data. *Forum for Linguistic Studies*, 5(3):1904–1920.

Kumar, D., Kumar, S., & Joshi, A. 2023. Assessing the viability of blockchain technology for enhancing court operations. *International Journal of Law and Management*, 65(5):425–439. https://doi.org/10.1108/IJLMA-03-2023-0046.

Lebese, J. 2013. The undefined role of court interpreters in South Africa. Dissertation submitted in accordance with the requirements for the degree of Master of Arts in Translation Studies at the University of South Africa.

Liu, J. 2022. The impact of technologies on interpreting: An interpreter and trainer's perspective. *International Journal of Chinese and English Translation and Interpreting*, 1:1–8. https://doi.org/10.56395/ijceti.v1i1.14.

Lopes, A. J. 2004. *A Batalha das Línguas: Perspectivas sobre Linguística Aplicada em Moçambique/ The Battle of the Languages: Perspectives on Applied Linguistics in Mozambique*. Maputo: Imprensa Universitária.

Lourens, C. 2012. Language rights in the constitution: The 'unborn' language legislation of subsection 6(4) and the consequences of the delayed birth. In C. Brohy, T. du Plessis, J. G. Turi & J. Woehrling (eds.). *Law, Language and the Multilingual State. Proceedings of the 12th International Conference of the International Academy of Linguisitc Law*. Stellenbosch: African Sun Media.

Lungu, P. 2025. Manifestation of power in the discourse of lawyers and witnesses in the Malawian courtroom. In Docrat, Z., De Vries, A., Kaschula, R. H., & Svongoro, P. (eds.). *Courtroom Discourse: Practical Insights from Legal Linguists*. Stellenbosch: Sun Press. 81–98.

Lwara, E., Kondowe, W., & Ndalama, D. 2024. Entrenching effective multilingualism in Malawian courtrooms through interpreting services: What do we learn from the 2019 presidential elections case? In Kondowe, W. Kamanga, C. M. M, & Madula, P. (eds). *Multilingualism in Southern Africa: Issues and Perspectives*. New York: Routledge. 122–142.

Mabasso, E. 2019. Tell us the story in your Portuguese, we can understand you: The Mozambican justice system's dilemma in enforcement of the sole official language policy in Mozambique. In Ralarala, M. K., Kaschula, R. H., & Heydon, G. (eds.). *New Frontiers in Forensic Linguists: Themes and Perspectives in Language and Law in Africa and beyond*. Stellenbosch: SUN PRESS. 33–48).

Mabasso, E. & Heydon, G. 2022. Mozambican police interviews: The interaction between official language and legal pluralism. In Ralarala, M. K., Kaschula, R. H., & Heydon, G. (eds.). *Language and the Law: Global Perspectives in Forensic Linguistics from Africa and beyond*. Stellenbosch: African Sun Media. 37–61. www.jstor.org/stable/j.ctv2svjxpj.11.

Malan, J. J. K. 2009. Observations on the use of official languages for the recording of court proceedings. *Tydskrif vir die Siud Afrikaanse reg (TSAR)*, 1(1):141–155.

Maphosa, R. & Nhlapo, N. 2020. Transformative legal education in the South African context. *Pretoria Student Law Review*, 14(1): 12–30. https://doi.org/10.29053/pslr.v14i1.1846.

Masiangoako, T. 2019. Rationalizing injustice: The reinforcement of legal hegemony in South Africa. *South African Crime Quarterly*. 66: 7–18. https://doi.org/10.17159/2413-3108/2018/v0n66a5633.

Matende, T., Svongoro, P., & Munyaka, T. 2022a. How does the work environment affect court interpreters working in Zimbabwe's magistrates' courts? *Journal for Translation Studies in Africa*, 3. https://doi.org/10.38140/jtsa.v3i.6630.

Matende, T., Mugari, V., & Gotosa, K. 2022b. Language and the legal process in deaf communities: An analysis of sign language court interpretation and linguistic rights of the deaf in selected courtrooms in Harare Urban, Zimbabwe. *London Journal of Research in Humanities and Social Sciences*. 22(9):23–35.

Mkhulisi, N. & Du Plessis, T. 2001. Managing multilingualism in SADC. In Deprez, K., Du Plessis, T. & Teck, L. (eds.). *Multilingualism, the Judiciary and Security Services: Belgium, Europe, South Africa, Southern Africa*. Pretoria: Van Schaik. 153–167.

Modupe, A., Celik, T., Vukosi Marivate, V. & Olugbara, O. 2022. Post-authorship attribution using regularized deep neural network. *Applied Sciences*. 12(15):7518.

Moeketsi, R. 1999a. *Discourse in a Multilingual and Multicultural Courtroom: A Court Interpreters' Guide*. Pretoria: van Schaik.

Moeketsi, R. H. 1999b. Redefining the role of the South African court interpreter. *Proteus*, 8(3–4): 12–15.

Moeketsi, R. & Mollema, N. 2006. Towards perfect practice in South African court interpreting: A quality assurance and quality management model. *International Journal of Speech Language and the Law.* 13(1):76–88. https://doi.org/10.1558/sll.2006.13.1.76.

Moeketsi, R. & Wallmach, K. 2005. From spaza to makoya! A BA degree for court interpreters in South Africa. *The International Journal of Speech, Language and the Law*, 12(1):77–108.

Mulayim S., Lai, M., & Norma, C. 2015. *Police Interviews and Interpreting: Context, Challenges, and Strategies*. London: CRC Press.

Muraguri, P. & Satia, E. 2023. Ranking of descriptors for complainants based on perceived victimhood: A case of written opinions in the Tanzanian court of appeal. In Kaschula, R. H., Ralarala, M. K., & Heydon. G. (eds.). *Language, Crime and the Courts in South Africa and beyond*. Stellenbosch: Sun Press. 137–156.

Muraguri, P., Nganga S., & Satia E. 2024. An examination of the terms used to describe sexual assault in written judicial opinions from the Tanzanian court of appeal. *MUST Journal of Research and Development*, 5(3):832–844.

Mustafa, M. 2020. *Analyzing Stance in Online Threat Discourse by Anti-Immigration Attackers: An Integrated Approach*. Cairo: American University in Cairo.

Muza, V. 2008. Zimbabwe: Transform Court Language Policy. *Financial Gazette Newspaper*, 13 September.

Mwangi, P. W., Kiguru, G., & Nthiga, P. 2022. 'The witch made me do it!' A speech act analysis of the provocation defence in witch lynching cases in Kenya. In Ralarala, M. K., Kaschula, R. H., & Heydon, G. (eds). *Language and the Law: Global Perspectives in Forensic Linguistics from Africa and beyond.* Stellenbosch: African Sun Media. 203–220.

Namakula, C. S. 2019. When the tongue ties fair trial: The South African experience. *South African Journal on Human Rights*, 35(2):219–236. https://doi.org/10.1080/02587203.2019.1615383.

Namakula, C. S. 2023. *Fair Trial Rights and Multilingualism in Africa: Perspectives from Comparable Jurisdictions*. New York: Routledge. ISBN 9781003325819 (ebook).

Ndatyapo, N. N. 2022. A forensic linguistic investigation of witness statements on murder cases at Windhoek police station. In Namibia University. MA thesis. Namibia University of Science and Technology.

Ndlovu, E. 2020. Interpretation and translation as disciplines and professions in Zimbabwe: A critical appraisal. *Language Matters*, 51(2):129–147. https://doi.org/10.1080/10228195.2020.1773518.

Ndlovu, E. 2023a. The open court principle in Zimbabwe: A language rights perspective. *Southern African Linguistics and Applied Language Studies*, 42(2):150–163. https://doi.org/10.2989/16073614.2023.2226176.

Ndlovu, E. 2023b. The right to an interpreter in the Zimbabwean justice system: The missing link. *Journal of African Languages and Literary Studies*, 4-(1):17–45. https://doi.org/10.31920/2633-2116/2023/v4n1a2.

Ngogo, L. 2025. The Application of ICT in Safeguarding the Rights of Suspects during the Police Interview in Tanzania; Law and Practice. *East African Journal of Law and Ethics*, 8 (1): 14–26. https://doi.org/10.37284/eajle.8.1.2600.

Ngubeni, B. 2023. Navigating multilingualism in the South African justice system: Challenges and solutions for accurate interpretation in South African courts. *De Rebus*. www.derebus.org.za/navigating-multilingualism-in-the-south-african-justice-system-challenges-and-solutions-for-accurate-interpretation-in-south-african-courts/.

Ngure, E. W. M. & Nganga, S. 2022. Men as vulnerable disputants in the Kikuyu traditional elder's courts. In Ralarala, K. M., Russell H. K., & Georgina, H. (eds.). *Language and the Law: Global Perspectives in Forensic Linguistics from Africa and beyond*. Stellenbosch: Sun Press. 361–374.

Nosilela, B. 2020. Making South African tertiary education multilingual: The implementation, monitoring and evaluation of SANTED Multilingualism Projects 2007 – 2010. Unpublished PhD thesis. Makhanda: Rhodes University.

NyaKaunda Kamanga, D. (2025). The application of language and procedural entitlements of children in detention in Malawi. In Kondowe, W. & Svongoro. P. (eds.). *Discrimination and Access to Justice in Africa: Language, Vulnerability and Social Inclusion in Southern and Eastern Africa*. New York: Routledge. 60–76.

Nyati-Ramahobo, L. 2001. Multilingualism in the judiciary and security services in Botswana. In Deprez, K., Du Plessis, T. & Teck, L. (eds.). *Multilingualism, the Judiciary and Security Services*: Belgium, Europe, South Africa, Southern Africa. Pretoria: Van Schaik Publishers. 177–188.

Nyirenda, A. K. C. 2014. The role of the judiciary in protecting the rights of vulnerable groups in Malawi. Paper presented at the Judicial Colloquium on the Rights of Vulnerable Groups, held at Sunbird Nkopola Lodge, Mangochi, Malawi, on 6 and 7 March 2014.

Odhiambo, G. F. & Daniel, O. O. 2023. Terrorism threat notes as criminal speech acts: A corpus based approach. In Kaschula, R. H., Ralarala, M. K., & Georgina, H. (eds.). *Language, Crime & Courts in Contemporary Africa and beyond*. Stellenbosch: African Sun Press. 203–222.

Odhiambo, K., Kavulani, C. K., & Matu, P. M. 2013a. Court interpreters' view of language use in subordinate courts in Nyanza Province, Kenya. *Theory & Practice in Language Studies*, 3(6):910–918.

Odhiambo, K., Musyoka, E. N., & Matu, P. M. 2013b. The impact of consecutive interpreting on church sermons: A study of English to Kamba interpretation in Machakos town, Kenya. *International Journal of Academic Research in Business and Social Sciences*, 3(8):189–204.

Odhiambo, G. F., & Orwenjo, D. O. (2023). Terrorism threat notes as criminal speech acts: A corpus-based approach. In R. H. Kaschula, K. R. Monwabisi, & H. Georgina (eds.). *Language, crime and courts in contemporary Africa and beyond*. Stellenbosch: African Sun Media.

Oguejiofor, N. E. & Evbuomwan, O. O. 2022. A survey of forensic linguistic services in Nigerian policing and judicial process. *International Journal of Forensic Linguistics*, 3(1):116–123. https://doi.org/10.22225/ijfl.3.1.4112.116-123.

Olsson, J. 2008. *Forensic Linguistics: An Introduction to Language, Crime and the Law*. 2nd ed. London: Continuum.

O'Nyangeri, A., Habwe, J., & Omboga, Z. 2022. Witness or Interpreter? *International Journal of Translation, Interpretation and Applied Linguistics*, 4(1):1–20. https://doi.org/10.4018/ijtial.314790.

Pereira, C. F. 2023. Mozambican Courts and International Law. *Communities and Collections-Faculdade de Direito (FD)*. http://hdl.handle.net/10362/165534.

Perry, T. 2004. *Language Rights, Ethnic Politics: A Critique of the Pan South African Language Board*. Cape Town: PRAESA Occasional Papers No. 12. https://bit.ly/3oCVGb7.

Poshai, L. & Vyas-Doorgapersad, S. 2023. Digital justice delivery in Zimbabwe: Integrated electronic case management system adoption. *South African Journal of Information Management*, 25(1):1–11, a1695. https://doi.org/10.4102/sajim.v25i1.1695.

Quinot, G. 2024. Developments in comparative public law in South Africa. *Droit Public Comparé*. https://doi.org/10.35562/droit-public-compare. 119: 1–22.

Ralarala, M. K. 2014. Transpreters translation of complainants' narratives as evidence. Whose version goes to court? *The Translator*, 20(3): 377–395.

Ralarala, M. K. 2017. Language and law: "cultural translation" of narratives into sworn into statements. In Kaschula, R., Maseko, P. & Wolff, H. E. (eds.).

Multilingualism and Intercultural Communication: A South African Perspective. Johannesburg, South Africa: Wits University Press. 211–222.

Ralarala, M. K & Lesch, L. T. 2022. Police intralingual translations of complainants' statements in South Africa: From interviewing to collaborative record construction of a legal text. In. Ralarala, M. K., Kaschula, R. H. & Heydon, G. (eds.). *Language and the Law: Global Perspectives in Forensic Linguistics from Africa and beyond*. Stellenbosch: African Sun Media. 15–35.

Ralarala, M. K & Rodrigues, T. 2019. Incarcerated, incriminated or vindicated? Na investigation into socio-pragmatic elements of police interviewing. In M. K. Ralarala, R. H. Kaschula & G. Heydon. *New Frontiers in Forensic Linguists: Themes and Perspectives in Language and Law in Africa and beyond*. Stellenbosch: Sun Press. 15–32.

Ralarala, M. K. and Lesh, L.T. 2022. Police intralingual translation of complainant's statements in South Africa: From interviewing to collaborative record construction of a legal text. In Ralarala, K. M., Russell H. K., & Georgina, H. (eds.). *Language and the Law: Global Perspectives in Forensic Linguistics from Africa and beyond*. Stellenbosch: Sun Press. 15–35.

Ralarala, M. K., Kaschula, R., & Heydon, G. 2022. *Language and the Law: Global Perspectives in Forensic Linguistics from Africa and beyond*. Stellenbosch: African Sun Media https://public.ebookcentral.proquest.com/choice/PublicFullRecord.aspx?p=29383226.

Ranosa-Madrunio, M. & Martin, I. P. 2023. *Forensic Linguistics in the Philippines: Origins, Developments, and Directions*. Cambridge: Cambridge University Press.

República de Moçambique. 2019. Lei da Revisão do Código Penal. Lei n.° 25/2019. Maputo: Imprensa Nacional de Moçambique. https://bit.ly/3vhBylZ [Accessed 10 December 2024].

Satia, E. 2012. Language and the construction of a positive identity among inmates in Kenyan jails. *Proceedings of The International Association of Forensic Linguists'* Tenth Biennial Conference. Birmingham: Centre for Forensic Linguistics. 92–103.

Satia, E. 2013. Strategies of controlling the linguistic response from cross-examined witnesses: Lay defendants as cross examiners in a Kenyan resident magistrate's court. *The University of Nairobi Journal of Languages and Linguistics*, 3:28–51.

Satia, E. & Kembo-Sure. 2017. Language crimes: The grammar and vocabulary of hate speech in Kenya. *Mwanga wa Lugha*, 21–38.

Satia, E. & Maritim, R. 2022. Power and meaning in the *Kaaburwo*: A traditional court among the Arror of Kenya. In Ralarala, K. M., Russell H. K., & Georgina, H. (eds.). *Language and the Law: Global*

Perspectives in Forensic Linguistics from Africa and beyond. Stellenbosch: Sun Press. 375–394.

Soko, T., & Kondowe, W. (2025). Whose access to justice? Civil Procedure Rules and the Right of Access to Justice for Persons with Disability in the High Court of Malawi. In Kondowe, W., and Svongoro. P. (eds). *Discrimination and Access to Justice in Africa: Language, Vulnerability and Social Inclusion in Southern and Eastern Africa*. New York: Routledge. 79–94. https://doi.org/10.4324/9781003569435-8.

South African Government. 1996. The Constitution of the Republic of South Africa Act No. 108 of 1996.

Stern, L. 2011. Courtroom interpreting. In Malmkjaer, K. & Windle, K. (eds.). *The Oxford Handbook of Translation Studies*. Oxford: Oxford University Press. 325–342.

Svongoro, P. 2024. The challenges faced by Zimbabwe's universities in Forensic Linguistics (FL) education and the promises stakeholders can make to address the challenges. *Documenting Forensic Linguistics in the African Context: Perspectives in Language and Legal Practice*. Stellenbosch: Sun Press.

Svongoro, P. & Kadenge, M. 2015. From language to society: An analysis of interpreting quality and the linguistic rights of the accused in selected Zimbabwean courtrooms. *Southern African Linguistics and Applied Language Studies*, 33(1):47–62. https://doi.org/10.2989/16073614.2015.1023501.

Svongoro, P. & Kondowe, W. (2024). An evaluation of Zimbabwe's advancements in the field of judicial interpreting in multilingual courtrooms. In Kondowe, W, Chimwemwe, M.M & Madula, P (eds.). *Multilingualism in Southern Africa: Issues and Perspectives*. London and New York: Routledge. 143–162.

Svongoro, P. & Wallmach, K. 2019. Interpreters' treatment of questions during consecutively interpreted interactions in Zimbabwean courtrooms. *South African Journal of African Languages*, 39(3):324–329. https://doi.org/10.1080/02572117.2019.1672344.

Svongoro, P. & Wallmach, K. 2022. The challenges of technical sight translation in criminal proceedings: Insights from English-Shona trials in Zimbabwe. In Ralarala, M., Kaschula, R. H., & Heydon, G. (eds.). *Language and the Law: Global Perspectives in Forensic Linguistics from Africa and beyond*. Stellenbosch: Sun Press. 145–162.

Svongoro, P. & Ralarala, M. K. (2023). Zimbabwe's constitutional safeguards for persons with communication disabilities: Implications for access to justice. In Ralarala M.K., Kaschula R.H & Heydon G (Eds). *Language, Crime and Courts in Contemporary Africa and Beyond*. Stellenbosch: Africa Sun Media. 147–169.

Tomblin, S., MacLeod, N., Sousa-Silva, R., Coulthard, M., & Nini, A. 2012. Proceedings of the International Association of Forensic Linguists' Tenth Biennial Conference. Centre for Forensics Linguistics, Birmingham.

Triki, N. 2013. Narratorial techniques in Tunisian police and court transcripts: A forensic linguistic approach. In *Text and Context*. Imprimerie Officielle de la République Tunisienne. E-Journal of Linguistics. 219–251.

Tyeng'o, M., Kembo-Sure E., Lonyangapuo, M., Satia, E., & Ogada, R. 2015. Performative in Kenyan Courtroom Discourse. *Research on Humanities and Social Sciences*, 5. ISSN (Online) 2225-0484. www.liste.org. 209–216.

Umiyati, M. 2020. A literature review of forensic linguistics. *International Journal of Forensic Linguistics*, 1(1):23–29. http://doi.org/10.22225/.2.1.1603.1-6.

Umiyati, M. 2021. Evolution of forensic linguistics publication: From a Europe and North America continent (1980–2021). *International Journal of Arts and Social Science*, 5(9):51–58.

Usadalo, S. E. & Kotzé, E. 2015. Communicative challenges of interpreting in cross-border languages in South African courtrooms. *South African Journal of African Languages*, 35(1):57–65. https://doi.org/10.1080/02572117.2015.1056464.

Usadolo, S. E. 2010. Justice through Language: A critical analysis of the use of foreign African Interpreters in South African Courtrooms. Port Elizabeth: Unpublished DPhil Thesis in African Language Studies at NMMU.

van Niekerk, G. (2015). Multilingualism in South African courts: The legislative regulation of language in the Cape during the nineteenth century. *Fundamina*, 21(2), 372–391. https://doi.org/10.17159/2411-7870/2015/v21n2a10

Verheul, J. 2020. 'Rotten Row is Rotten to the Core': The Material and Sensory Politics of Harare's Magistrates' Courts after 2000. *Polar Political and Legal Anthropology Review*. 43(2):262–279. https://doi.org/10.1111/plar.12376.

Wambura, B. J. 2023. The cut: Women and the practice of female genital mutilation in Kuria, Kenya. In McNiff, J. (ed.). *Representations of the Academic*. New York: Routledge. 120–134.

Wambura, B. J. & Satia, E. 2023. Language and ideology in Kuria female genital mutilation (FGM) songs. In Kaschula, R. H., Ralarala, M. K., & Heydon, G. (eds.). *Language, Crime and Courts in Contemporary Africa and beyond*. Stellenbosch: African Sun Media. 157–178.

Yi, O. 2023. Interpreting questions in courtroom examinations: A study of English-Mandarin Chinese interpretations of question types in remote settings. *Translogos Translation Studies Journal*. 6(2): 1–42. https://doi.org/10.29228/translogos.58.

Zergat, K. Y., Selouani, S. A., Amrouche, A., Kahil, Y., & Merazi-Meksen, T. 2023. The voice as a material clue: A new forensic Algerian corpus. *Multimedia Tools and Applications*, 82(19): 29095–29113.

Zikhali, W. 2019. Community Policing and Crime Prevention: Evaluating the Role of Traditional Leaders under Chief Madliwa in Nkayi District, Zimbabwe. *International Journal for Crime, Justice and Social Democracy*, 8(4): 109–122.

Zoloni, M. & Ndalama-Mtawali, D. 2025. Legal status of Malawi sign language: Implications on language rights and access to justice for the deaf. In Kondowe, W. & Svongoro, P. (eds.). *Discrimination and Access to Justice in Africa: Language, Vulnerability and Social Inclusion in Southern and Eastern Africa*. New York: Routledge. 188–203.

Selected Case law

AfriForum NPC v *Chairperson of the Council of the University of South Africa and Others* 2020 ZASCA 79 (30 June 2020).

M Oosthuizen *and A Van Straten* v *The State* (2024)*State* v *Damoyi* 2004 (1) SACR 121 (C).

State v *Damani* 2016 (1) SACR 80 (KZP).

State v *Gordon* 2018 ZAWCHC 106 (29 August 2018). https://doi.org/10.1093/ejil/chy068 *State* v *Lesaena* 1993 (2) SACR 264 (T).

State v Leseana 1993 (2) SACR 265 (T).

State v *Manzini* 2007 (2) SACR 107 (W).*State* v *Matomela* 1998 (3) BCLR (Ck).

State v Ndala 1996 (2) SACR 218 (C).

State v *Pistorius* 2016 ZAGPPHC 724.*State* v *Siyotula* 2003 (1) SACR 154 (E).

State v *Van Breda* 2018 ZAWCHC 87 (7 June 2018).

State v *Matomela* 1998 (3) BCLR (Ck).

State v *Ndala* 1996 (2) SACR 218 (C).

State v *Pistorius* 2016 ZAGPPHC 724.

State v *Siyotula* 2003 (1) SACR 154 (E).

State v *Van Breda* 2018 ZAWCHC 87 (7 June 2018).

Acknowledgement

This work is based on research supported by the National Heritage Council (NHC). Opinions, findings, conclusions, and recommendations expressed in this publication are those of the authors, and the NHC accepts no liability in this regard.

Cambridge Elements

Forensic Linguistics

Tim Grant
Aston University

Tim Grant is Professor of Forensic Linguistics, Director of the Aston Institute for Forensic Linguistics, and past president of the International Association of Forensic Linguists. His recent publications have focussed on online sexual abuse conversations including *Language and Online Identities: The Undercover Policing of Internet Sexual Crime* (with Nicci MacLeod, Cambridge, 2020).

Tim is one of the world's most experienced forensic linguistic practitioners and his case work has involved the analysis of abusive and threatening communications in many different contexts including investigations into sexual assault, stalking, murder, and terrorism. He also makes regular media contributions including presenting police appeals such as for the BBC Crimewatch programme.

Tammy Gales
Hofstra University

Tammy Gales is Professor of Linguistics and the Director of Research at the Institute for Forensic Linguistics, Threat Assessment, and Strategic Analysis at Hofstra University, New York. She has served on the Executive Committee for the International Association of Forensic Linguists (IAFL), is on the editorial board for the peer-reviewed journals Applied Corpus Linguistics and Language and Law / Linguagem e Direito, and is a member of the advisory board for the BYU Law and Corpus Linguistics group. Her research interests cross the boundaries of forensic linguistics and language and the law, with a primary focus on threatening communications. She has trained law enforcement agents from agencies across Canada and the U.S. and has applied her work to both criminal and civil cases.

About the Series

Elements in Forensic Linguistics provides high-quality accessible writing, bringing cutting-edge forensic linguistics to students and researchers as well as to practitioners in law enforcement and law. Elements in the series range from descriptive linguistics work, documenting a full range of legal and forensic texts and contexts; empirical findings and methodological developments to enhance research, investigative advice, and evidence for courts; and explorations into the theoretical and ethical foundations of research and practice in forensic linguistics

Cambridge Elements⹀

Forensic Linguistics

Elements in the Series

Forensic Linguistics in the Philippines
Marilu Rañosa-Madrunio, Isabel Pefianco Martin

The Language of Fake News
Jack Grieve, Helena Woodfield

A Theory of Linguistic Individuality for Authorship Analysis
Andrea Nini

Forensic Linguistics in Australia: Origins, Progress and Prospects
Diana Eades, Helen Fraser, Georgina Heydon

Online Child Sexual Grooming Discourse
Nuria Lorenzo-Dus, Craig Evans and Ruth Mullineux-Morgan

Spoken Threats from Production to Perception
James Tompkinson

Authorship Analysis in Chinese Social Media Texts
Shaomin Zhang

The Language of Romance Crimes: Interactions of Love, Money, and Threat
Elisabeth Carter

Legal-Lay Discourse and Procedural Justice in Family and County Courts
Tatiana Grieshofer

Forensic Linguistics in China: Origins, Progress, and Prospects
Yuan Chuanyou, Xu Youping and Lu Nan

Decoding Terrorism: An Interdisciplinary Approach to a Lone-Actor Case
Julia Kupper, Marie Bojsen-Møller, Tanya Karoli Christensen, Dakota Wing, Marcus Papadopulos and Sharon Smith

Forensic Linguistics in Southern Africa: Origins, Progress, and Prospects
Russell H. Kaschula, Monwabisi K. Ralarala, Eliseu Mabasso, Zakeera Docrat, Wellman Kondowe, and Paul Svongoro

A full series listing is available at: www.cambridge.org/EIFL

For EU product safety concerns, contact us at Calle de José Abascal, 56–1°,
28003 Madrid, Spain or eugpsr@cambridge.org.

www.ingramcontent.com/pod-product-compliance
Lightning Source LLC
LaVergne TN
LVHW011854060526
838200LV00054B/4327